# Long Island's
## *Gold Coast Elite*
### AND
# THE GREAT WAR

# LONG ISLAND'S
## *Gold Coast Elite*
### AND
# THE GREAT WAR

RICHARD F. WELCH

THE
History
PRESS

Published by The History Press
Charleston, SC
www.historypress.com

First published 2021

Manufactured in the United States

ISBN 9781467147033

Library of Congress Control Number: 2021934593

*For Shirley Marie Welch*
*1921–2005*

# CONTENTS

# ACKNOWLEDGEMENTS

As always, I have been aided by many people whose support, encouragement and expertise made this book possible. Thanks to Laura Cinturati and Susan Sarna at Sagamore Hill, Iris Levin at the Nassau County Museum system and Victoria Aspinwall of the Long Island Studies Institute for providing many key illustrations. Likewise, let me extend my appreciation to Paul Hunchak, education coordinator at Old Westbury Gardens; Carol Stern of the Glen Cove Library's Local History Room; and Karen Martin, archivist at the Huntington Historical Society, for making materials from their extensive photographic collections available. I am indebted to Chris Ryon, Port Jefferson Village historian, for designing the map of the Gold Coast for this book. I wish also to thank the staff of the Northport Public Library for tracking down materials not readily accessible in most public collections.

A special note of gratitude is due historians and authors Bill Bleyer and Libby O'Connell and research assistant Carolyn Price for taking on the job of critiquing the book in its earlier guises.

Finally, thanks to the staff at The History Press, especially Banks Smither, who approved and encouraged this project, for guiding its final transformation into a published work.

Suffice it to say, any flaws or errors remaining are solely those of the author.

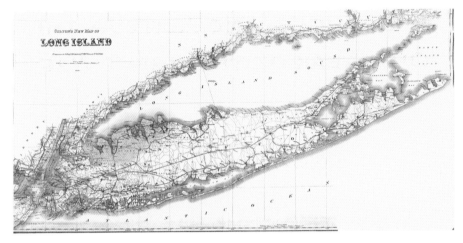

Long Island showing the approximate extent of the Gold Coast (*shaded area*), circa 1890–1940. *Courtesy of Chris Ryon, Port Jefferson Village historian.*

# THE LONG ISLAND ELITE AT THE OUTBREAK OF THE GREAT WAR

*A*t the outbreak of the First World War in 1914, the United States was a militarily weak, self-identifying neutral nation whose people were largely reluctant to intervene in the conflict that had exploded among the major European powers. By 1917, the nation had been radically transformed. The increasingly threadbare cloak of neutrality had been discarded for fully engaged belligerency, the country's industrial might stoked by the near-bottomless demands of the war and a majority of its citizenry enthusiastically enlisted in the cause of Allied victory. This shift in attitude and policy during the three years between 1914 and 1917 bore tremendous consequences, as the American entry into the war, coming when it did, and on the side it did, decided the outcome.

Many factors played a role in this transformation. But among the key elements that produced this dramatic turnabout was the commitment of a small but highly influential network of people who embraced the Allied—specifically Anglo-French—cause early on. This key group of major players spent its immense social, economic and political capital in an unrelenting campaign to induce its government and its countrymen to shed attempts at neutrality and non-intervention and adopt the policy of complete military, financial and economic support for the Allies arrayed against Germany.

Were they the most important people in the American effort in the Great War? Certainly not in numbers. Nor, when the United States entered the conflict, did they possess a greater quotient of courage, talent or commitment to the war effort than laborers, farmers or middle-class professionals.

Nevertheless, this relatively small cohort of Americans exerted an outsized influence in the shaping of American attitudes and public policy prior to the United States' official entry into the war. Between 1914 and 1917, the privileged old stock elite, epitomized by Long Island's Gold Coast families, succeeded in tilting American government policy and financial resources to the benefit of the Allies. In doing so, America's economic interests became so intertwined with those of Britain and France that an open break with Germany became increasingly unavoidable. Moreover, they deployed their celebrity and social prominence to inspire and exhort—where they did not push—the wider American public to enlist in the war effort both "Over Here and Over There."

They did one more thing. Having played a conspicuous role in the United States' gradual but inexorable march into the war, they showed no hesitation in supporting the national crusade at home and participating on the battlefront when the opportunity finally came. In sum, the history of the Gold Coast society and its role in the First World War explains much about how the nation entered and fought the war that marked its emergence as a world power.

# Chapter 1

# The Gold Coast in 1914

*I*n the years between 1870 and 1920, the North Shore of Long Island attracted a disproportionate chunk of the wealthiest, most prestigious families in the nation. Some of these were second- or third-generation members of families who had made their mark and their fortunes in the earlier enterprises dating from just before and after the Civil War. They were joined by the more newly, almost unfathomably rich, whose numbers increased as the forces of industrialization and technological innovation transformed the nation and the world. These were the families of men who had made their money in the great enterprises of the industrial age—steel, coke, petroleum, railroads and the insurance, banking and financial firms that made them possible and expanded their reach. Their economic power was matched by social prominence and distinction. They advertised their status through location of residence, material displays of wealth as exemplified by the mansions they had built and the careful selection of elite preparatory schools and Ivy League institutions for their children's education. While never numerous, this privileged elite dominated the nation's economy and the governmental and social hierarchy and basked in the admiring, envious or hostile gazes of their less affluent countrymen.

# THE NORTH SHORE

Dubbed the Gold Coast for the sizable number of wealthy families residing there—the 1 percent if not the 0.1 percent of their times—Long Island's Gold Coast grew from two major sources: proximity to Manhattan and the natural attractions of its North Shore. Most of the wealthy Gold Coast figures did their business at corporate headquarters in Manhattan and likewise maintained their fashionable urban residences in New York City. New York summers were often brutally hot, however, and many well-off New Yorkers had begun to summer in gentler, more bucolic settings even before the Civil War. Long Island, stretching 120 miles from the East River to Montauk Point, was a frequently chosen destination. Ready access to Manhattan, provided by the Long Island Rail Road, steamships, private yachts and later by improved roadways and automobiles, gave Long Island a comparative advantage over more distant—or less well-connected— areas and offered a practical inducement to those seeking an alternative to city living.

There was the deeper draw of the Island's natural beauty. Outside Brooklyn and Long Island City, Long Island in the circa 1880–1920 period remained largely rural. This was particularly true of the North Shore, the area roughly between the City Line (the border between the Borough of Queens and Nassau County) and Port Jefferson some thirty miles to the east, in Suffolk County. Long Island Sound forms the northern border, and the area extends southward to approximately Jericho Turnpike (Route 25) or, geologically, the southern edge of the Harbor Hill/Ronkonkoma moraine junction. The area boasted scenic, fjord-like bays and harbors, girded by wooded hillsides, orchards and farmland. The topography offered ample opportunities for equestrian sports as well as boating, yachting, fishing or simply, to use a term of the time, "rusticating," usually in a carefully designed, man-made facsimile of nature.

Beginning around 1880,[1] wealthy businessmen or their children—equally affluent and often endowed with more leisure time—began acquiring property on the necks of land extending into Long Island Sound. Another favored locale, Old Westbury, which lay farther inland, drew wealthy families with what, to outsiders at least, seemed its Currier & Ives character. Smaller bastions of the Industrial Revolution's wealthy classes sprung up along the south shore of Suffolk County and in what was beginning to be known as "the Hamptons." These areas drew those whose recreational interests were focused on the Great South Bay.

Most of the new estates were carved from existing farms; often, several were purchased and combined for the purpose. On occasion, preexisting structures—and occasionally a small village—were removed and the reminders of the area's previous usage obliterated. In their place rose imposing mansions or country houses whose owners sometimes misleadingly labeled them "cottages." Many of the period's best-known architects were recruited to design houses suitable for the lords of finance and industry. The estate or country houses drew from a wide array of styles, though the great Georgian mansions of Britain and their American analog, the Federal style, were probably the most common sources of inspiration. As financier and North Shore resident Henry P. Davison later put it, "In my opinion there is no place in the world where such comfort exists as in an English country house."[2] The creation of imposing estates advertised both the desirability and exclusivity of an area, which, in turn, rendered it attractive to additional well-heeled families, resulting in ultra-upscale communities of affluent power brokers.

The proliferation of country houses or mansions was dramatic. Between 1865 and 1939, 975 estates were built between the City boroughs and Montauk Point. In the process, Long Island emerged as the epicenter of American affluence, and the North Shore, increasingly referred to as the Gold Coast, became the nation's premier prestige address.[3] This transformation was well chronicled in the press. In 1902, the *New York Herald* reported, "Long Island is rapidly being divided up into estates of immense acreage…beyond all precedent of American country life….Nowhere else in America, possibly the world, are to be found so many great landed estates in a similar area."[4]

The socioeconomic nature of the North Shore and like parts of Long Island were radically altered by the new monied arrivals, as farmlands and existing patterns of community life—often extending far back into the colonial past—were altered beyond recognition. But as the earlier methods of work and monetary pursuit were lost, new ones appeared. The Gold Coast families, though relatively few in number, employed sizable workforces drawn heavily from local inhabitants. In addition to architects and landscape designers, construction of the estates required various types of labor—bricklayers, carpenters, stonemasons and the like. They, in turn, procured necessary materials from local or regional suppliers. Gardeners converted the landscape designer's plans into reality and kept the grounds in prescribed condition. Nurseries sprang up that sold to the public but whose main income was derived from estate owners or managers. Maids, butlers, footmen, chauffeurs, gamekeepers, cooks, grooms and stable keepers were among the many staff members necessary to maintain the great houses in proper running order. For the locals, spending by the Gold Coast elite could constitute a major income stream.

Further employment might be had at the private clubs that the recent arrivals established in pursuit of their sporting interests, pastimes that had been a major draw to the Island from the beginning. A 1916 publication, *Prominent Residents of Long Island and Their Pleasure Clubs*, counted seventy-one clubs east of Queens "whose members participate in Fox Hunting, Polo, [horse or automobile] Racing, Golf, Tennis, Aviation, Yachting, Fishing, Hunting etc."[5] Often designed by the same architects who created the great estates, clubhouses were impressive in their own right. *Country Life*, required reading on the Gold Coast, described the Piping Rock Club, established in 1911, as "the sort of thing George Washington would have built if he had the money."[6]

To secure and protect their phenomenally upscale neighborhoods, the Gold Coast families eventually turned many of them into incorporated villages, which allowed them to control land-use zoning, mandate the minimum size of property and outlaw unwanted commercial activity. Incorporated villages such as Kings Point, Sands Point, the Brookvilles, Mill Neck, Matinecock, Lattingtown, Oyster Bay Cove, Laurel Hollow, Old Westbury, Lloyd Harbor and Old Field soon occupied the most desirable stretches of land on the

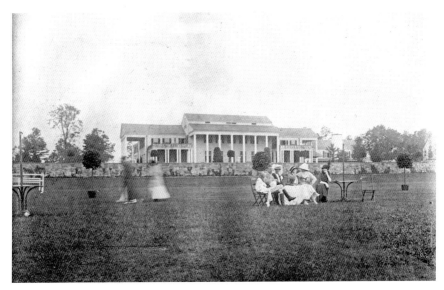

The Piping Rock Club, circa 1910. *Courtesy of the Nassau County Museum Photographic Archive.*

Peacock Point, Lattingtown. *Courtesy of the Nassau County Museum Photographic Archive.*

North Shore. Monied families sometimes simply created estate districts in larger, unincorporated areas, such as the Pratts and Morgans did in Glen Cove. In such circumstances, they relied on their juice with the local zoning committees to preserve the character of their neighborhoods.

The process of site selection and estate creation is illustrated by the experiences of Harry P. Davison. Davison, a key member of J.P. Morgan and Sons, chose Peacock Point in Lattingtown for his Long Island home shortly after joining the bank in 1909. The location had much to recommend it. In addition to the Long Island Sound frontage, Peacock Point was an easy commute to Wall Street and conveniently lay only about two miles from the Morgan estate, Matinecock Point, on East Island in Glen Cove. (Indeed, the Morgan bank's local presence was further deepened by the residence of partner William Porter, also in Glen Cove, and, shortly after the war, partner and munitions chief Edward R. Stettinius.)

Peacock Point possessed the usual accoutrements of upscale country living—mansion house, tennis courts, polo fields, gardens and the like. When the original house burned down in 1912, Davison took advantage of his shoreline frontage and outfitted a luxury houseboat with electricity, telephone service and running water. The well-accoutered and provisioned craft, tethered to a pier, served as the family residence while the new house

Shoreline at Peacock Point. *Courtesy of the Nassau County Museum Photographic Archive.*

was built.[7] The waterfront also provided an anchorage for the commuter yachts he sometimes used to convey him to his office in downtown Manhattan.[8] During the war it would be put to other uses as well. As his close friend and colleague Thomas W. Lamont remembered, "Peacock Point became [Davison's] permanent home and held his devoted interest as long as he lived."[9]

While the Gold Coast's cachet as a prestigious setting for upscale families extended to all professions, it seems to have been particularly alluring to the banking and financial sector—and not just the Morgan clique. In 1911, Robert Low Bacon, son of Theodore Roosevelt's secretary of state and Taft's ambassador to France, purchased a house and grounds in Old Westbury that he dubbed "Old Acres." Though the family originated in Massachusetts, Bacon chose Long Island for its proximity to his office with the Kissell-Kinnicut and Co. investment bank in the city. Other areas might do as well in terms of distance, but the Gold Coast held pride of place among suitable communities for the elite, as well as offering congenial social and recreational networks that often doubled as informal business and political alliances as well.

Neither Davison nor Bacon was an outlier. Jay Phipps and Thomas Hitchcock in Old Westbury, Henry Stimson in West Hills, William K.

Vanderbilt in Centerport and, most famously, former president Theodore Roosevelt at Sagamore Hill were among the many wealthy, powerful and influential people who came to view their Long Island estates as not just places to "rusticate" but their true homes.

By the 1920s, when F. Scott Fitzgerald wrote of this "riotous, slender Island," the recently established monied classes had remade the North Shore in line with their own ideals of esthetics, status and utility. As North Shore historian Robert B. MacKay observed, "The barrier island, the agrarian outpost which had been passed over by the industrial revolution for lack of falling water to power mill turbines, was suddenly the most desirable residence in the United States, with capital, connections, and infrastructure of social services, utilities, and employment opportunities that had seemed unattainable just a generation earlier."[10]

The movers and shakers of the day succeeded in imposing their vision of home, society and community on the North Shore. The Gold Coast was their achievement. How they might use their muscle to affect American foreign and military policy during the first great conflagration of the twentieth century would soon be demonstrated.

## CHAPTER 2

# TAKING SIDES

"We wanted the Allies to win from the onset of the war. We were pro-Ally by inheritance, by instinct, by opinion."[11] The "we" in this statement by Morgan banker Thomas W. Lamont were the wealthy, old stock members of his professional and social class, and this well describes the response of the Gold Coast families. As Amos S. Pinchot, Progressive Party politician and brother of Theodore Roosevelt's forestry commissioner, succinctly put it, "The [pro]war party is also essentially a moneyed and leisure class party."[12]

Some members of the area's leading families were immediately involved personally. The master of Westbury House (now Old Westbury Gardens), Jay Phipps, whose father had been Andrew Carnegie's partner, had a direct personal connection to the Allied cause. His sister, Amy, had married British politico Frederick Guest. The Guests opened their British homes to the government for use as a convalescent facility for wounded British soldiers. The regular correspondence between London and Old Westbury gave Phipps and his family an intimate view of the war from the British point of view. When the United States entered the war in April 1917, Phipps and his estate would play a direct role in the country's new crusade.

Few single families had a more immediate and powerful impact on America's involvement in the war, both before and after its official entry, than that of Henry P. Davison, whose estate, Peacock Point in Lattingtown, was a short drive from the Morgan holdings in Glen Cove. Though J.P. "Jack" Morgan Jr. officially succeeded his father, the legendary J.P. Morgan, following his death in 1912, he was less involved in the mechanics and operations of the nation's largest financial institution than his father had been. Davison, who had been one of Morgan Sr.'s golden boys, stepped into the role of chief executive officer and de facto bank president.

Harry, as he was known to family and friends, had already earned his spurs as a financial wizard and was credited as the "architect" of the legendary (or notorious) Jekyll Island meeting that laid the groundwork for the establishment of the Federal Reserve System in 1913.[13] In the assessment of Thomas W. Lamont, fellow Morgan partner and close friend of Davison, "[I]f Mr. Morgan had been the ruler of a state, Davison would have been his prime minister."[14] In other words, while Jack Morgan reigned, Davison ruled.

J.P. "Jack" Morgan Jr. *Courtesy of the Glen Cove Public Library, Robert R. Coles Long Island History Room.*

Davison's motives were mixed but always committed to the Allies, especially the British interest. Like many in American business and politics, he believed war would be avoided until the moment it broke out.[15] But once hostilities commenced in August 1914, he unhesitatingly placed his proven talents for organization and finance at the service of the British war effort, which he, along with most of his ethno-economic strata, considered equally beneficial to American prosperity and his understanding of a transatlantic Anglo-Saxon hegemony.[16] As Lamont boasted, "In J.P. Morgan & Company's office, from the first of August, 1914, all were heart and soul for the Allies, and of all the partners Davison was the most fertile in new ideas.…Here was a chance for the firm…to render the Allies a great service by coordinating their purchases and bringing orderliness to their methods. He sensed also that an orderly development of those purchases would mean great opportunity, great expansion, great prosperity for American manufacture and the whole of the American business community."[17] And no part of that community would be in a position to prosper more than the financial house that made the necessary arrangements.

Davison, Lamont and Jack Morgan immediately moved to put their sentiments and interests into action. They made no secret of their sympathies and brazenly flouted the Wilson administration's formal call for "genuine neutrality." Of course, by design or obliviousness to likely consequences, Wilson had opened the door to the bankers when he and his advisors refused to embargo American arms trade, claiming the right of freedom of the seas. In any event, encouraged by pro-Allied politicians and public figures in and out of government, under Davison's leadership, J.P. Morgan and Sons turned American neutrality into a threadbare cloak and the United States into the Allies'—especially the Anglo-French component—larder, arsenal and bank.

In November 1914, Davison sailed to London, where he opened high-level talks with British officials that resulted in J.P. Morgan and Sons being designated the United Kingdom's official agent for procurement in the United States. In the process, Harry Davison effectively became a lobbyist, or agent of influence, advising the British government on political developments in the United States.[18]

Certainly, Davison, Lamont and their compatriots believed that America's interests—economic as well as political—ran roughly parallel to those of Britain. From their perspective, aiding the British and, to a more limited degree, France ultimately aided the burgeoning power of the United States.[19] That Britain controlled the sea lanes was also a practical consideration. Nevertheless, the bank's activities increasingly sapped the official policy of neutrality, including Wilson's ability to maneuver, as "financial matters involving the House of Morgan and the Allies...became so tangled and complex that only an expert in international finance with full documentation could discern precisely what transpired."[20]

Davison also spearheaded the efforts of the Morgan bank to provide funding for the Allied war effort, which would allow them to purchase war material in the United States and through which Morgan would receive a commission for his services. Initially, most members of the Wilson administration opposed loans for the Allies—or any belligerents—but Davison, aided by sympathetic figures in the administration, got around that by having the loans rebranded "bank credits." Benjamin Strong, first governor of the New York Federal Reserve Bank, played a key role in the administration's reversal of its loan policy. A Morgan ally, Strong had been urged by Davison to accept the key post, and he, in turn, persuaded the Wilson administration that its anti-loan policy was undesirable.[21] In August 1915, the combined pressure from both the Morgan bank and the Fed led Wilson to drop his opposition to public loans for the belligerents. Nevertheless, he remained uneasy about such loans and would not endorse them openly.[22]

Master of the Universe, Harry P. Davison, circa 1918. *Courtesy of the Library of Congress.*

Between March and October 1915, Morgan, leading or pressuring other banks, secured $160 million in bank credits to the Allies, primarily Britain and France. In October 1915, Davison floated another $500 million (all in 1914–19 dollars) for the Anglo-French cause.[23] Between 1915 and 1917, Morgan floated Allied loans totaling $1,400,000,000 on the American market. The Morgan partners sold an additional $886,000,000 in repatriated American securities for Britain and assorted Allied nations.[24]

The costs of fighting a modern, industrialized war were so enormous that even Morgan's prodigious efforts on its behalf proved insufficient for Britain's requirements. In November 1916, Davison met with Wilson and the Federal Reserve Board in Washington. Already endowed with an abundance of self-confidence, the banker had become more imperious as a result of his high-level dealings with chancellors and prime ministers, and it was on full display at the meeting.[25] Davison informed the president and the nation's money masters that Morgan Bank intended to issue at least $10 million unsecured British Treasury notes per week, possibly up to a total of $1 billion.[26] If the government refused to permit such a loan, he told the president, Britain and France would flood the United States with gold, which would trigger a massive inflation. Davison's announcement, essentially a demand for acquiescence and endorsement, was too much for Wilson and the Federal Reserve Board. His refusal to compromise on the matter only stiffened their opposition to his virtual ultimatum.[27]

Administration opposition intensified after the press reported that the Federal Reserve Board had endorsed the scheme—which it had not. The board then informed Davison that if he did not delay the issue of the new massive loans, the government would publicly deny its alleged approval. They were fully supported by Wilson, who calculated that the Allies' financial predicament would make them more receptive to a new peace proposal he was preparing to launch.[28] Davison dug in his heels and refused to budge.

The Fed and the president called Davison's bluff. On November 28, the Fed sent a round robin message to member banks plus—on Wilson's initiative—private investors, warning them against "foreign treasury bills of this character."[29] Stung, Davison's first instinct was to ignore the announcement and push ahead with his new loan campaign. He also proposed to the British that the Allies cut back on purchases of American material. His idea was to squeeze the United States economically, which would threaten the economic boom driven by the manufacture and sales of war-related material to the Allies.[30] The proposal calls into question whether or not Davison and his partners had come to value the interests of the Allies, and their bank, above those of the nation.

In addition to being "temperamentally…[unable] to accept failure or indeed moderate success," as he confessed in a moment of self-awareness, Davison's obstinate behavior may have been influenced by yet another factor: fear.[31] In order to keep British wartime financing going, the Morgan Bank had established an unsecured "call [or demand] loan." But British financial needs were so steep that it was impossible for the bank to continue to pile up such debt for more than a brief time.[32] For their part, the British believed that without the continuous injection of American money, their ability to continue the war would be exhausted in an equally short period. This may indeed have been part of the calculations of the Federal Reserve Board and Woodrow Wilson himself. United States financial pressure would force the belligerents to the negotiating table, where the American president would be arbiter.[33]

Indeed, the American market for Allied securities was effectively dead between November 1916 and April 1917, with Britain and France scrambling for financing and heavily dependent on the Morgan Bank's "demand loan." A chastened Davison kept a low profile during this dicey period for both the Allies and the bank and "conveniently vanished on an extended vacation in early 1917."[34] Meanwhile, the British, who had no wish to antagonize Wilson, sent their own financial representatives to the United States to deal with the now volatile issue of American financing.[35]

In any event, the Germans unwittingly resolved the crisis by reinstituting unrestricted submarine warfare, which enflamed American grievances, caused the reversal of the administration's previous opposition to loans to the Allies and, in a little over a month, took the United States into war.

Whatever the full intentions of the administration might have been during the November imbroglio, Davison's ill-thought-out threat to advise the Allies to boycott American manufacturers was both counterproductive and economically impossible. The British were dependent on American financing of 10 million pounds per day, as well as an uninterrupted supply of American war material.[36] The crisis was relieved by the United States' official entry into the war in April 1917. The Wilson administration then opened the treasury's spigots, ultimately extending $7.1 billion in financial aid to the Allies by November 1918.[37]

Nevertheless, although administration officials assumed the direction of American financial and economic aid, they often found it expedient—when not necessary—to turn to the Morgan bankers for advice and guidance. The connections and experience that the Morgan bankers had gained in the 1914–17 period proved invaluable and near irreplaceable. No other group possessed both the personal connections and detailed knowledge required to negotiate with America's European allies.[38]

The Morgan Bank did far more than arrange financial backing for the Allies. In January 1915, in order to consolidate Allied purchasing in one agency, Davison created an autonomous Export Department specifically charged with procuring arms and war materials.[39] Believing the Morgan Bank lacked necessary experience in running such an operation, Lamont and Davison recruited Edward Stettinius to head the new venture. Stettinius, a native of St. Louis and president of the Diamond Match Company, among other enterprises, moved to New York in 1905 and settled with his wife and four children on a thirteen-acre estate on Dongan Hills, Staten Island.[40]

Stettinius took over the Export Department on January 15, 1915. The following month, Davison wrote, "We are more than pleased with the way the work has progressed so far, and particularly pleased with Stettinius who

Edward R. Stettinius, munitions czar. *Courtesy of the Library of Congress.*

has shown himself to be quite a remarkable man."[41] In fact, Davison was impressed enough by the Export Department's head that at the end of 1915, he recommended Stettinius be made a partner in the bank, a suggestion that was seconded by Lamont and approved by Jack Morgan.[42]

Indeed, Stettinius was so effective that in 1916, Davison and the Morgan partners believed him to be at risk of kidnapping or assassination by German agents. The increasing dependence of the Allies on American material and money had not gone unnoticed by Germany, which sought to impede their flow. In 1916, a huge explosion destroyed a shipping pier at Black Tom, a small peninsula almost directly opposite the Statue of Liberty on the New Jersey shore. An enormous supply of munitions destined for Britain was waiting to be loaded when the entire area was nearly leveled by a bomb or bombs. Though the German hand in the destruction was not confirmed until the 1930s, there was little doubt at the time that the Kaiser's saboteurs were responsible.

Fearing the loss of his key arms procurer, Davison moved Stettinius to the power launch *Margaret*, which was moored in New York Harbor. Stettinius's family was relocated from Staten Island and rented first in Southampton and then in Locust Valley on Long Island.[43] From this point, Stettinius was increasingly drawn into the Gold Coast milieu, a status that he would make permanent after the war. To make his sojourn on the yacht more comfortable, Davison personally furnished the vessel, choosing the antiques and décor he thought appropriate for a Morgan partner.[44]

"The Chief," as Stettinius was called by his staff of 175 men, pushed himself and the Export Department hard. While he was known for his consideration and efficiency, he was equally famous for "his indifference to the clock." The Export Department worked all hours and sometimes on Saturdays. To maintain morale and show his appreciation, Stettinius sometimes rewarded the SOS ("Slaves of Stettinius") with dinners at New York's tonier restaurants.[45] In a magazine interview, Stettinius extolled his workers' commitment, stating, "I have never before in my life known such sustained, white heat enthusiasm, such determination to get things done, such disregard of personal convenience and comfort, such self-sacrifice."[46] Hyperbole aside, under the Chief's leadership the Export Department proved remarkably effective, and he himself a remarkably efficient executive.

Stettinius divided the Export Department into categories: large-caliber ammunition, propellants, explosives, heavy chemicals and food. For his lieutenants, those who oversaw the subdivisions and scouted out suitable companies to award contracts, he preferred engineers and manufacturers to businessmen.[47] Nor were small arms neglected, as Morgan bankers arranged for British loans to keep firearms manufacturers Winchester, Remington and Eddystone (a Remington subsidiary) turning out rifles for the Allies.[48]

Stettinius worked in close coordination with the British War Office to expedite and rationalize Allied purchases. For their part, the Allies offered "almost irresistible terms" for contractors who were well aware the arrangements had the clout of the Morgan Bank behind them.[49] All in all, Davison and Stettinius created a private arms and munitions industry that could rival that of many nations and was greater than that of the United States government at the time. Such sales turned the American economy from recession in 1914 to boom by 1915, a transformation that could not be ignored by politicians hoping to remain in office.[50]

Though at one point the British suggested distributing contracts geographically, the Export Department worked mostly with a few major corporations. The big four were DuPont, Bethlehem Steel, United States Steel and American Smelting and Refining. These alone accounted for nearly one-third or $1 billion in contracts made through the Export

Department.[51] Charging a 1 percent commission on all its purchases, the Morgan Bank netted $30 million for its services to the Allies.[52] Ironically, despite his proven expertise and ability, Stettinius was not given any major role in government purchases after the United States officially entered the conflict in April 1917. Although appointed an assistant secretary of war, he was bounced from one assignment to another, treatment that may have resulted from a suspicion of the Morgan Bank felt by influential people in the Wilson administration.[53] Nevertheless, for Davison, Lamont and Stettinius, once the United States entered the war on April 6, 1917, their primary agenda was fulfilled.

The decision by Davison and the Morgan partners to secure Stettinius on a guarded yacht in New York Harbor might seem an overreaction, but events close to home provided ample motivation. In addition to the operations of German saboteurs and the denunciations of non-interventionists, pacifists and socialists, the Morgan bankers and their allies had learned that their prominence (or notoriety) made them targets of those who held them personally responsible for the slaughter in Europe.

On July 3, 1915, a man initially identified as Frank Holt, recently an instructor of German at Cornell University, arrived at Jack Morgan's estate on East Island in Glen Cove. He carried with him two revolvers and two sticks of dynamite, part of a larger supply that he had used to set off a bomb in the Senate Reception Room in Washington the night before.[54] With no security at the entrance to the island, which must be reached by a short causeway, or the house itself, Holt simply pressed the bell and, when the door opened, tried to bluff his way past the butler. When that failed, he pulled his pistols and pushed in.

At the time, Morgan was breakfasting with his wife and the British ambassador, Cecil Spring Rice, and his wife. The butler succeeded in sending Holt to the wrong part of the house, thus buying time. But the intruder soon made his way up the stairs, where he found Morgan's younger children and, pointing a pistol at them, told them to follow him down the second-floor hallway. At that point, he finally encountered Morgan and his wife, who had been alerted to possible danger by the butler's cries. "I've got you, Mr. Morgan!" Holt shouted, but he was the one who was got. Morgan unexpectedly lunged at Holt, forcing him to the floor and pinning him with his 220-pound bulk.[55] Nevertheless, the would-be assassin got off two shots. One .38-caliber bullet passed through the banker's thigh, and another struck him in the abdomen. With Holt held virtually immobile by Morgan and Morgan's wife, the pistols were pried from his hands. Other

Matinecock Point from the air, circa 1930. *Courtesy of Old Long Island.*

servants quickly appeared and began beating Holt on the head with the butts of the revolvers. The butler cracked him over the head with a piece of coal until he was well bloodied and near unconscious.[56]

The local justice of the peace and Glen Cove's chief of constables soon arrived and replaced the ropes that the staff had used to restrain Holt with handcuffs. He was then taken away to the Glen Cove Courthouse. In the meantime, still wounded and bleeding, Morgan walked to his bedroom and called his doctor. He then phoned his New York office, briefly reported what had happened and assured them he was not seriously hurt. Luckily, he was not. Harry Davison dispatched two specialists from New York on his yacht to Glen Cove. They agreed the wounds were not life threatening.[57] Fortunately for Morgan, both bullets had passed through his body and were retrieved, obviating the need for a dangerous probing operation.[58] Morgan spent his entire convalescence at his Matinecock Point home and would be back in his office in six weeks.

"I wanted to get Mr. Morgan to use his influence to stop the exportation of arms….I only meant to scare him," Holt explained to the lawmen.[59] Indeed, he was very talkative, almost anxious to explain himself to both the authorities and reporters at the Glen Cove lockup and later following his transfer to Nassau County facilities. While he gave different versions of his intentions, he largely kept to his story that he was tormented by the carnage in Europe and obsessed by the American role in providing the means of the death and destruction.

Holt's story became increasingly elaborate as more information surfaced. Though he never adequately explained what he intended to do with the dynamite he was carrying, he claimed his main objective was to hold Morgan's wife and children hostage until the "all-powerful Mr. Morgan" induced arms and munitions manufacturers to halt operations.[60] In a letter he wrote his wife in Dallas on July 2, which she received four days later, Holt admitted he was the R. Pearce who had sent letters to the president and public officials claiming credit for the bomb that detonated in a Senate reception room that night. Though the device caused considerable damage, no one was injured. The letter also laid out his planned operation in Glen Cove. He needed, he said, "a powerful assistant [to halt arms trade] and I have chosen J.P. Morgan." If Morgan didn't convince arms manufacturers to stop, he went on, "he must forfeit his family....If the rich of this country wish to get richer by the European horror, they must also be ready to participate in the horror."[61]

Overall, Holt stuck to his story regarding his motives and intentions. In an interview with Dr. Carlos F. MacDonald, an alienist (psychiatrist) brought in to examine him by Nassau County, Holt returned to the crucial element of munitions shipment and war. Asked if he thought he had a legal right to attack Morgan, the prisoner replied that his actions had "nothing to do with legal right. My dear sir, this is war." When the doctor protested that the United States was not at war, Holt countered, "You are wrong. We are at war. We are actually at war. We are killing thousands of people every day." "But we haven't declared war," the psychiatrist pointed out. "Yes," Holt retorted. "We are doing it underhandedly." MacDonald tried a new approach. "Do you think that you, single-handed, could arrest the trend of an age?" "No," Holt responded unhesitatingly, "but Mr. Morgan could."[62]

Holt's plan was fanciful at best. If he could have carried it further, he would only have succeeded in getting himself killed and perhaps causing the deaths of some members of Morgan's family and household. But the "trend of an age" would have continued unimpeded. Morgan was its obvious symbol. After all, the company that bore his name was the mainspring behind the faux neutral trade with the Allies. But if Holt had researched the issue more deeply, he would have seen that the controlling intelligence and energy behind the Morgan Bank's key role in buttressing Britain and France lived not at Matinecock Point on East Island but a mile and a half down the shoreline at Harry Davison's Peacock Point estate.

As for Dr. MacDonald, he concluded Holt was a "paranoiac of the reformatory type" whose mental confusion was demonstrated by "how he thought he could imprison the Morgans, barricade the door on them, and prevent their rescue by laying a stick of dynamite on the table."[63]

Both Nassau County police and detectives from the New York City Bomb and Anarchist Squad began to trace Holt's movements and soon discovered he had been a busy man. After finishing a semester teaching and completing his doctorate at Cornell, he checked into a Manhattan hotel but spent most of his time at a cottage he had rented in Central Park (Bethpage) on Long Island under the name of Patton. Using another false identity, C. Hendricks, he purchased dynamite from the Aetna Explosives Company in Long Island City and had it shipped to the Long Island Rail Road depot at Syosset, where he retrieved it. He assembled the bombs at Central Park and dispatched the unused explosives to a storage facility in Manhattan, where the police later discovered them.[64]

Holt purchased his two pistols at pawnshops in New Jersey and used the backyard of his cottage as a practice range. The shooting became so annoying that the neighbors discussed complaining to the police. But then it suddenly stopped as Holt began to activate his plan.[65]

Naturally, both law enforcement and the public were eager to understand not just Holt's motivations but also his connections—whether he had any confederates and whether or not he was part of a German-orchestrated conspiracy. Reporters and investigators visited Cornell, where friends and acquaintances described him as "decidedly pro-German," but not intemperate. Nor did they remember him being "engaged in any active propaganda." Colleagues recalled he "condemned the export of arms…to the warring nations of Europe because Germany didn't get a fair deal." Nevertheless, he had always seemed to express his opinions calmly, and his violent spree was attributed to overwork.[66] That conclusion of Holt's Cornell colleagues echoed that of the *Brooklyn Eagle* reporter who had interviewed him in Glen Cove. "There was nothing in the man's talk or words up to that time to give any indication that he was of unsound mind."[67]

There were undoubtedly many other questions reporters, police and prosecutors wanted to ask Holt—and the list was growing rapidly—but they never got the chance. On July 6, Holt killed himself outside his cell in the Nassau County lockup. It was his second attempt. After he had first tried to end his life by cutting his wrists with the metal band on an eraser, one of the jailers, Jerry Ryan, was assigned to watch him constantly. However, during the night, Ryan, according to his account, thought he heard a noise and stepped away from the cell, leaving the door open. Holt climbed the crossbars to the top of his cell and threw himself headfirst twenty feet onto the concrete floor.[68]

Though stories swirled about his death, especially since Ryan initially swore he had heard an "explosion," the official verdict was death from the fall. Holt's brain was removed for examination by an alienist and was kept in a pail until this could be arranged. His body, minus brain, was embalmed and shipped to Dallas, where his wife and family lived.[69] Before the transit could be arranged, and as news of the suicide spread across the country, new information revealed that Patton, Hendricks and Pearce were not the only pseudonyms the bombmaker-assassin employed. Frank Holt, however, was his most successful deception.

The Morgan assassination story was major news throughout the country, and most newspaper accounts ran photographs of Holt taken after his arrest. Almost immediately, people who knew him at Cornell and in his previous life in Cambridge, Massachusetts, identified him as Erich Muenter. Muenter, an instructor in German at Harvard, had disappeared in 1906 just as he was to be indicted for the murder of his wife by poison.[70] (Interestingly, some former acquaintances of Muenter's who met him as Holt before the Morgan escapade made no attempt to inform police authorities.)[71] He fled to Mexico, where he worked with the El Oro Mining and Rail Road Company before returning to the United States in 1908 under the identity of Frank Holt. Muenter resumed his old profession as language instructor, teaching at several colleges in Texas and the Midwest before arriving back east at Cornell.

But Muenter had left one last mystery for the bomb squad. In his July 2 letter to his wife, he revealed he had placed a bomb on a ship sailing for Britain with munitions but couldn't remember the name. He was sure, however, that the device would explode on July 7. Muenter's wife immediately turned the letter over to the authorities, and government agencies began radioing all vessels sailing from New York to be aware they might be carrying the explosive.

On July 7, the day after his presumed suicide, an explosion tore through the steamer *Minnehaha* as it cleared the East Coast of the United States. Fortunately, Muenter's dynamite satchel had been placed in storage away from the munitions the ship was transporting to Britain.[72] Nevertheless, serious fires erupted, which took the crew two days to extinguish while the captain sailed for Halifax.[73] There were no casualties, and the ship soon resumed its voyage successfully delivering a cargo of 2,800 cases of shrapnel shells, 1,723 artillery shells, 1,000 cases of cordite explosives, 1,400 cases of TNT, 3,000 barrels of motor oil, 60 hogsheads of rum and 230 horses for the Royal Artillery. There were also several hundred tons of food on board.[74] The voyage of the *Minnehaha*, one of hundreds of vessels supplying the western allies, offers a graphic illustration of the extent of the American munitions trade. The Morgan Bank also supplied the ship itself. The *Minnehaha* was registered to the International Merchant Marine, a Morgan subsidiary.[75]

Perhaps the ultimate question connected with the attempted Morgan assassination revolved around whether or not Holt/Muenter was a German agent. German intelligence was active in the United States at the time, desperately trying to halt or reduce the flow of supplies to the Allies as well as keeping the United States from entering the war on their side. By the spring of 1915, German saboteurs had managed to set off a number of incendiary devices on ships headed for Allied ports, causing seventy fires or explosions that resulted in thirty-eight killed and $22 million in damages.[76] The German underground network's greatest success was the destruction of the Black Tom shipping depot in the early morning of July 30, 1916, which caused $20 million in damages and left five dead.[77] Even with Black Tom, the efforts of German agents had minimal effect on the torrent of arms, munitions and food being shipped to the Allies.[78]

But was Muenter one of them? He was probably born in Germany in 1871 and had immigrated to the United States by 1890. He was likely sympathetic to Germany when the Great War began, as were many German Americans. However, few of them joined German espionage cells or shrank from supporting the war effort after Wilson took the United States into open conflict with Germany. Nor is there any evidence that Muenter was recruited by German intelligence during the war. Thomas Tunney, head of New York City's Bomb and Anarchist Squad, which played a major role in combatting German sabotage, conceded that "the entirety of the plot could never be known."[79] He nevertheless doubted Muenter had the ability to construct an effective bomb by himself and questioned where he obtained the funds necessary to execute his plans.[80]

In the absence of direct evidence, the most likely conclusion is that Muenter was what today is called "self-radicalized." His sympathies in favor of his ancestral homeland were likely inflamed by indignation and outrage over the financial and arms support to Britain and the Allies arranged by Davison, Stettinius and their partners. Muenter's personal history—the murder of his first wife—also reveals a willingness to resort to violence, which, in turn, suggests a twisted, volatile mental state. If any others were involved in Muenter's plot, they covered their tracks well, and dead men tell no tales.

The near assassination of the country's leading banker led to changes on the North Shore. Now aware there was a downside to their high-profile material and vocal support of the Allies, many of the most prominent among them implemented heightened security measures. The caution demonstrated by Stettinius's sojourn on the Morgan yacht was matched by Jack Morgan's deployment of thirty guards around the approaches to East Island. Clarence Mackay, whose estate, Harbor Hill in Roslyn Harbor, was once considered the most opulent on Long Island, applied to the local justice of police for a permit to carry a pistol.[81] Wealthy Oyster Bay residents, unnerved by Muenter's plot, requested the formation of a new police district in their area, reporting "many burglaries and incendiary fires over the past year with no arrests."[82] No longer could an unknown individual approach the Morgan house, Matinecock Point, or any of the other Gold Coast and Old Westbury mansions. For the Gold Coast, the war was drawing closer.

## CHAPTER 3

# VOLUNTEERS

*W*hile most Gold Coast families blessed with deep pockets and financial connections lavishly provided money and material to the Allies, others lent their support through more prosaic and often more personal ways.

Large numbers joined the Commission for Relief in Belgium, headed by a young Herbert Hoover. Almost all of Belgium, except a small sliver in its northwest, fell under German occupation in 1914. Subject to the demands of the German occupiers and blockaded by the British navy, the civilian population suffered the pangs of deprivation early in the war. To alleviate this situation, both sides allowed the Commission for Relief in Belgium to ship supplies of food and other necessities into the distressed nation. Benefiting from an effective public relations campaign, branches of the commission were established across the nation raising funds for food, clothing and medical supplies. Though both the Germans and Allies had cooperated in the commission's activities, the fact that Belgium was under German military occupation and administration gave the commission's activities a pro-Allied tint. Additionally, the membership was dominated by Allied sympathizers, though Hoover's leadership was both even-handed and effective.

Some Americans were already in Europe when the war broke out and became immediately involved. Amy Guest, older sister of Jay Phipps—whose residence, Westbury House, was and remains one of the jewels of Long Island—married British politician Frederick Guest before the war and had settled into her adopted country. Once hostilities commenced, she actively promoted women's service in the war effort and led a women's march of fifty thousand participants through the streets of London in 1915. She was also instrumental in organizing the Wounded Allies Relief Committee and lent her London home, Aldford House, as a Red Cross hospital for British servicemen. When the United States joined the war, Aldford House's mission was extended to include wounded American naval personnel.

Harry Davison's devotion to the Allied cause was shared by all members of his family, including his two sons, Trubee and Harry Jr. Trubee, a student at Yale, took the lead in wartime involvement. In the summer of 1915, he accompanied his father on one of the latter's frequent trips to Europe arranging financial and material support for the Allies. While there, Trubee volunteered for the American Ambulance Service, which conveyed wounded British and French troops from the front lines to the better-equipped hospitals in the rear.

Robert Bacon and Richard Norton were the primary movers behind the creation of the Ambulance Americaine and its counterpart, the American Volunteer Ambulance Corps, commonly called the American Ambulance Service (AAS). Bacon, an Old Westbury resident, had served as assistant secretary of state during the presidency of his Harvard classmate Theodore Roosevelt and was a former member of Morgan and Drexel, the Morgan Bank's Philadelphia branch. Norton was the son of Harvard professor Charles Eliot Norton. As the AAS took shape, volunteer drivers, stretcher bearers and other staff were recruited from college campuses, initially Harvard.[83] Financial backing came from a number of prominent Long Island families, including William K. Vanderbilt II, who owned Eagle's Nest overlooking the Sound in Centerport. Vanderbilt provided the cash for the AAS's ten cars and later paid for the first Nieuport aircraft flown by the Lafayette Escadrille.[84]

When he returned to Yale in the autumn, Trubee continued to support the AAS by raising funds for the service. In 1916, Harry Jr. drove for the AAS in France, while his brother remained in America trying to get a more ambitious project literally off the ground.[85]

Trubee's stint in France had whetted his appetite for deeper involvement. In particular, the exploits of the Lafayette Escadrille, an American volunteer unit flying with the French air force, inspired his decision to enlist the family name, connections and resources in the creation of a naval aviation squadron, which he saw as a necessary corrective to a glaring weakness in American defense. By 1916, he was beginning to put his plan into reality.[86]

But neither Trubee nor the other members of the American Ambulance Service were the first of their countrymen to render direct aid to the western

Ethel Roosevelt, circa 1910.
*Courtesy of Sagamore Hill National
Historic Site, National Park Service,
Oyster Bay, New York.*

Allies. That distinction went to members of what most would deem the "First Family of Long Island"—at least politically. Theodore Roosevelt, ex-president, noted naturalist, explorer and advocate of a strong national defense, shared the pro-Allied, anti-German sentiments of most of the North Shore elite—and indeed, that of the eastern, college-educated, financial and political establishment. An early advocate of American intervention in the war, he became increasingly strident, bellicose and intemperate in expressing his views, often in the form of vitriol unleashed against the Wilson administration, whose official adherence to neutrality stoked his ire and contempt.

Roosevelt's sentiments were echoed by his children, four boys and two girls. It was Roosevelt's younger daughter, Ethel (1891–1977), and her husband, physician Richard Derby, who were the first of the family, and among the first Americans, to reach France after hostilities broke out. The French had made a hospital in the Lycée Pasteur available to Americans impatient to aid the Allied cause. The six-hundred-bed hospital became the Ambulance Americaine hospital, and its directors asked U.S. universities for professional personnel to staff it for terms of six months. The Derbys and six other doctors signed on and sailed for France in September 1914.[87] Derby and Ethel, doctor and nurse, possessed just the skills the hospital sought to treat the rapidly growing numbers of casualties. While Trubee Davison and the other young AAS drivers brought in the wounded from the front, American medical teams like Dick and Ethel sought to save their lives.

The young couple returned to the United States aboard the *Lusitania* in December 1914, but their involvement in the pro-Allied and interventionist activities did not cease. Ethel remained active in wounded and refugee relief. In 1915, while still in America, she became "chairman" of the American Hospital for Refugees in Paris and organized a horse show to raise money for the cause.[88] Dick, as family and friends called him, joined the Preparedness Movement.

# PREPAREDNESS

The American support for the Allied nations, particularly Britain and France, was not only critical for their ability to wage war but also transformed the American economy and the political/international landscape. Between 1914 and 1916, American exports to the Allies totaled $7 billion, of which $2 billion derived from munitions sales.[89] The remainder came from sales of foodstuffs, cotton, raw materials, metals and the like. Much of this was organized by Harry Davison at the J.P. Morgan Bank.[90] Further evidence of American dependence on wartime trade can be seen in the near doubling of agricultural exports from 1915 to 1916.[91]

As a result of trade with the Allies, the United States went from a recession in 1914 to prosperity in 1915, the economic boom continuing until the end of the war. The dependence of the economy on such trade acted as a heavy brake on any serious attempt to maintain genuine neutrality despite the administration's stated position. Harry Davison himself conceded that "America's prosperity of today has been built upon war orders and particularly orders for munitions."[92] As historian Andrew Bacevich has observed, the aggressive agenda of the captains of finance and industry combined with the instincts and objectives of the administration to produce "an approach to 'neutrality' that mortgaged American prosperity to Anglo-French victory."[93] The growing accumulation of wealth and economic prosperity sometimes weighed on the consciousness of the younger members of the Gold Coast establishment who felt guilt that their nation's good fortune derived from the blood and pain of the warring nations—at least that of the Allies. Their response was not to call for American impartiality and an end to the export of war materials and financial support, but for the United States to enter the war openly on the Allied side.

The American aid to the Allies and its importance to their ability to fight did not go unnoticed by the Germans. At the outbreak of hostilities in 1914, the British imposed a naval blockade on Germany with the intent, in the words of Winston Churchill, First Lord of the Admiralty, to "starve the whole [German] population—men, women and children, old, young, wounded and sound—into submission."[94] The blockade virtually cut off American trade with Germany. Some of the British economic warfare methods were themselves violations of American neutrality and claims of freedom of the seas, but none provoked a critical crisis between the nations nor impeded the flow of American money and material.

What did cause increasing tension was the German deployment of a relatively new weapon, the *unterseeboot*, or submarine, usually referred to as a U-boat. German submariners attacked and sank British and Allied vessels, which often carried American passengers or merchant sailors, as well as supplies. The Wilson administration took the position that the presence of neutral citizens on British ships made them off-limits to German attacks. The sinking of vessels without warning by U-boats was also deemed a violation of the rules of war by both Britain and the United States.

The torpedoing of the British passenger liner *Lusitania* in 1915, resulting in the loss of 1,200 passengers, about 120 of whom were Americans, led to an outburst of outrage on the part of pro-interventionists. Theodore Roosevelt excoriated Wilson's attempt to resolve the dispute diplomatically as craven. On the other hand, Wilson's first secretary of state, William Jennings Bryan, noted the one-sided nature of interventionist anger. "Why be shocked at the drowning of a few people," he asked, "if there is no objection to starving a nation."[95] The remark went largely unnoticed. Bryan soon resigned and was replaced by the blatantly pro-Allied interventionist Robert Lansing. Though Wilson had managed to keep the country out of the war—at least directly— which helped secure his reelection in 1916, he was himself committed to aiding the Allies and securing a central position for himself and the United States at any peace conference.[96]

By 1915, supporters of intervention on the Allied side had embraced the cause of "Preparedness." The Preparedness Movement was a response to the well-understood deficiencies in the American military. The army consisted of approximately 120,000 men, with an additional 40,000 men enlisted in the state National Guards, whose training was often more wishful thinking than anything else. Even combined, these numbers were clearly inadequate for service in the modern, industrialized struggle raging in Europe. The navy was slightly better prepared, but air services were miniscule, and for all the munitions and rifles being produced, the country lacked artillery, aircraft and even an adequate supply of machine guns, whose widespread use on the Western Front was a key contributor to the ballooning number of casualties.

Calls to expand the size of the army and increase military training had long been a goal of the commander of the army's Eastern District, General Leonard Wood. Theodore Roosevelt had been Wood's second-in-command during the Spanish-American War, and he enthusiastically supported Wood's Preparedness campaign, including its call for the establishment of volunteer training camps.[97] Former secretary of war Edward L. Stimson, whose "gentlemen's estate," Highhold, was situated in the West Hills section of Huntington, become another vocal advocate of the Preparedness agenda.

The first response to proposals for voluntary summer training camps came from young East Coast businessmen, who were quickly joined by large numbers of college-age men, primarily from Ivy League schools.[98] Theodore Roosevelt Jr.; his brother-in-law Richard Derby; and Robert Low Bacon, the elder Robert Bacon's son, were among the small group of fifteen who petitioned Leonard Wood to establish a "Businessmen's Camp" at Plattsburgh in 1915. Wood was happy to oblige, and the first camp hosted one thousand men, including Quentin and Archie Roosevelt.[99] Not surprisingly, the ex-president visited Plattsburgh, New York, where he was welcomed by Wood before meeting with Ethel, who had come to visit her husband, Richard Derby, who was training as a private. The remainder of his brood greeted him later in the day.[100]

The distinctly affluent cast of volunteers led to the program being tagged "Millionaires' Camps." The sobriquet, though widely rejected by both the organizers and the trainees, was nevertheless close to the mark. The camps were run by the army, which provided facilities and training, while the college men paid for their uniforms and privilege of receiving instruction in drill, marksmanship, marching and the like. Soon the "Plattsburgh

Movement," as the volunteer training agenda became known, spawned other volunteer military camps, again primarily in the Northeast. The overall objective was to train about 100,000 young men for positions as future officers in a vastly expanded army that would be required once the country inevitably entered the war.[101]

An early and vocal Preparedness advocate, Theodore Roosevelt extolled the presumptive beneficial effects of the camps on the American polity. "The military tent," he maintained, "where boys sleep side by side, will rank next to the public school among the great agents of democracy."[102] The principle was sound in theory, but in reality, the camp drew heavily from young men at the same class/educational level, and often the same families, as the leaders of the pro-Allied interventionist movement. The volunteer training camps also followed the army in practicing racial segregation. No black people, regardless of educational status, took part in the camp sessions held in 1915 and 1916. Plans for an African American training camp in 1917 were scrapped when the United States entered the war and Plattsburgh was converted into an officer training camp.

Long Islanders got an up-close look at the military training camps when one was established at Fort Terry on Plum Island just off Orient Point on the eastern tip of the Island's North Fork. The camp was primarily designed for secondary school students, the first time the army opened training to young men under eighteen. In July 1916, the ever-active ex-president Roosevelt visited Fort Terry, where he informed the trainees that "the man who isn't fit to fight for his country isn't fit to vote."[103] After exhorting the young men to reject the arguments of those "nice old women of both sexes"—the pacifists—he declared that a nation unprepared for war would likely suffer the fate of Belgium. His solution to the challenge was universal military service.[104]

Theodore Roosevelt's enthusiastic embrace of Preparedness overlapped with his rapprochement with the Republican "Old Guard." He had crossed the party regulars when he ran for president in 1912 on the Progressive or "Bull Moose" line, splitting the Republican vote and giving Woodrow Wilson the White House. Roosevelt's progressive inclinations were real enough, but they were overshadowed by his nationalism, and when war broke out in Europe, his pro-Allied interventionist views aligned less with his Progressive Party followers than they did with that of the GOP leadership.

TR's return to the Republican fold, and wider influence, was cemented at a March 31, 1916 luncheon at the Park Avenue home of Robert Bacon, who also owned a country house in Old Westbury. Bacon was head of the

National Security League, an organization devoted to increasing the size and quality of the American military. Wood, Elihu Root and TR's old ally Senator Henry Cabot Lodge were also in attendance.[105] Though no one took minutes and no memorandum was kept, the meeting clearly represented Roosevelt's total break from the Progressive Party and return to the fold.

Republicans—with few exceptions pro-Allied, pro-Preparedness, pro-intervention and anti-Wilson—were delighted to have their most popular and dynamic figure back on the team. Former Bull Moosers who had followed Roosevelt in 1912 were as crestfallen with his desertion as they were dismayed by his rejuvenated bellicosity. Some noted that the "Trust Buster" had closer ties with big business than was popularly assumed, numbering among his closest friends and political allies Elihu Root, Henry Stimson and Philander Knox, all corporate attorneys.[106] Amos Pinchot, one of the disillusioned antiwar Progressives abandoned by TR, made the connection and feared a new presidential term for Oyster Bay's most distinguished resident. "Roosevelt could be relied on [by prowar tycoons] in every way. He was fiercely pro-British and pro-Ally, so if he were elected the Morgan group [might feel] that its loans to the Allied governments would have whatever security came from the support of the White House."[107]

In the meantime, the Preparedness campaign gathered strength, adherents and confidence. As expected, Roosevelt had a lot more to say, especially about the Wilson administration, whose reluctance to take a more aggressive stand toward Germany he decried as pusillanimous. Addressing the volunteers at Plattsburgh in the summer of 1916 (where Archie, Quentin and Derby were again in attendance), he ripped into the administration's persistent, if nominal, adherence to neutrality. "America has played an ignoble part among nations," he declared, going on to denounce "college sissies" and men with "mean souls."[108] Feeding off his own rhetoric, he argued that the country should stand with Wilson "only so long as the President stands by the nation."[109]

Roosevelt's slam at the administration cost Wood his command of the army's eastern division. Wood and Roosevelt were well known as friends and allies who shared the same opinion of national needs and Wilson's deficiencies. Additionally, Wood oversaw the training camps and had invited Roosevelt to visit the trainees. Perhaps mindful of the old adage "revenge is a dish best eaten cold," Wilson stayed silent and bided his time. His opportunity would come.

Preparedness was a full family enthusiasm for TR's brood. Whatever advantages they enjoyed from being the president's son were matched by

Theodore Roosevelt as seen by non-interventionists. *Courtesy of the Library of Congress.*

a sense of civic responsibility and a negative attitude toward the Central Powers. Ted signed up directly for Plattsburgh in 1915, while Archibald "Archie" and Quentin were enlisted by their father. Archie, Ted and Quentin were back at Plattsburgh the following summer. Kermit was less often available, as he had taken a position with a bank in Buenos Aires.

Even among the affluent collegiates who dominated the 1,400 trainees at Plattsburgh there were perceived differences in status. Ted was pleased that about half the attendees were Harvard men, as his father and brothers had been. "I suppose some Yale men would fight if there was a war," he mused dismissively, "but it is clearer than ever that Yale is the great middle-class college, and the middle classes are not naturally gallant."[110] Yale men no doubt saw it differently.

Ted was still a young man with limited experience in the world when he wrote those lines. War and life experience would alter his snobbery, and he went on to amass an estimable record in governmental and military service, culminating with the Medal of Honor for his service as first general ashore on Omaha Beach during the Normandy invasion in World War II. While attending Plattsburgh, Archie and Ted were graded as potential officer material, and when the time came in 1917, the brothers would be with the first United States soldiers to reach France. Quentin, the youngest, and the always different Kermit followed later.

In addition to the training camps, advocates of an increased military attempted to stoke popular support for their agenda through public demonstrations, especially "Preparedness Parades." Primarily a northeastern phenomenon, these public demonstrations replete with marchers, bands, floats and banners were held in towns, villages and cities, extolling bystanders to enlist in their movement, pressure elected officials to beef up the American military and take a harder stand against alleged German atrocities on the high seas and occupied territories.

Some towns on Long Island, such as East Hampton and Huntington, organized Preparedness Parades of a modest size commensurate with the size of their communities. On March 31, 1916, General Leonard Wood addressed an overflow crowd of Preparedness supporters at the Star Palace Theater in Patchogue on Suffolk County's South Shore. Local companies of the National Guard escorted Wood from his hotel to the theater, where he told his listeners that "there is nothing voluntary about our obligation to the nation in a democracy in times of stress."[111] As he reached the conclusion of his speech, he enjoined the audience and the nation to "educate the child to know that the last drops of blood in its body must be poured out in defense of the land we love."[112] Wood's rousing performance was a major event for a modest-sized village on Long Island, but local rallies paled in comparison with those held in the major cities, especially New York.

In May 1916, the Preparedness leaders—primarily Republican, often Morgan-connected businessmen, like those who had founded the National Security League—staged a massive parade in New York.[113] Upward of 125,000 marchers participated, and it took twelve hours for them all to stride uptown.[114] According to the parade's grand marshal, Colonel Charles H. Sherrill, the event was a response to a call "by a few patriotic individuals… and the record breaking number of businessmen."[115] The participants were divided into sixty-two "divisions," mostly composed of civic, political and social organizations, including the Red Cross and Boy Scouts. Women's groups were well represented, with the 5,000-member Women's League for Self-Defense and Preparedness providing a contingent. Mostly Brooklyn socialites, the Women's League leaders boasted that "none but American women, whose allegiance to the United States is unquestioned, are admitted."[116]

But pride of place among the female marchers went to Eleanor Butler Roosevelt, Ted's wife, who led the Independent Patriotic Women of America, 1,200 white-clad women who stepped off near dusk. Her mother-in-law, Edith Kermit Roosevelt, and sister-in-law, Ethel Derby, followed in the ranks.[117] The ex-president himself did not attend. Instead, he kept a low profile and spent the day meeting and addressing Boy Scouts at Sagamore Hill in Oyster Bay.

But Theodore Roosevelt did more than advocate military camps and Preparedness Parades. In 1915, he helped the pro-intervention/pro-Allied networks tap into a new technology to spread their message. Hudson Maxim, a munitions developer and brother of Hiram Maxim, inventor of the Maxim machine gun, had written a book, *Defenseless America*, narrating the invasion and defeat of the United States by an unnamed but obvious power—Germany. Theodore Roosevelt's Oyster Bay neighbor, J. Stuart Blackton, a movie producer with the Vitagraph Film Company, undertook the task of converting the book into a major, nine-reel movie, *The Battle Cry of Peace*, which first screened in September 1915. Roosevelt endorsed the project enthusiastically and recruited General Leonard Wood, Admiral George Dewey and Secretary of War Lindley Garrison to lobby for its production and promote it when completed.[118]

The National Guard provided twenty-five thousand men for the combat scenes, and the film was spiced with appearances by Wood, former (and future) secretary of war Henry Stimson, Secretary of State Robert Lansing and former president William Howard Taft. TR himself declined to appear. His visual participation was unnecessary. The movie, depicting the defeat and occupation of the United States as a consequence of pacificism, broadcast his agenda, and his fingerprints, metaphorically at least, were all over the production. *The Battle Cry of Peace* proved a popular hit after its debut in September.[119]

Though the former president was the most conspicuous figure calling for Preparedness and, ultimately, intervention, Long Island's North Shore was home to another advocate, almost as famous. This was Henry Lewis Stimson, secretary of war during the Taft presidency and a keen admirer of TR. Perhaps not surprisingly considering his former position, Stimson was an outspoken proponent for an enlarged, modernized military based on universal military service.

The scion of another old-stock, upper-class family, Stimson was motivated by a fear of American vulnerability to attack by a modern power—Germany—and an ingrained sense of Anglo-Saxon comity. His attitudes toward Germany originated with his father, who had switched from Wall Street to medicine and went to study in Europe. He trained first in Germany but soon left for Paris. This was partly to avail himself of a chance to study with Louis Pasteur but also because he was "disgusted by the martial swagger of the youthful German Empire."[120] His father, Stimson recalled, had taught him to mistrust the Germans and admire the French.[121]

A recent secretary of war, Stimson was as familiar with the army's weaknesses as Wood or Roosevelt. As early as December 1914, he was publicly urging a program of Preparedness, and before a crowd of 1,500 members of the New York Merchant's Association, he described the country as "a great, helpless, unprepared nation."[122] An adamant supporter of Wood's Preparedness Camps, Stimson visited Plattsburgh in 1914 and 1915 and, despite being in his late forties, enrolled for training in 1916.[123] Like TR, who had launched him in his public career, Stimson was unrelenting in his calls for military preparedness and modernization, though he avoided taking personal jabs at Wilson.

In December 1915, Stimson pushed Preparedness as an "insurance policy against invasion."[124] After the war finally concluded, he predicted the United States would enjoy prosperity, while the European powers would be "beggared."[125] The resentful European nations, he argued, would not allow American prosperity to go "unchallenged." France, he claimed, despised the United States for its "wish-wash policy, England feels very strongly that we are not living up to our duty as Anglo-Saxons, and Germany feels very strongly that we are not giving her a square deal by supplying munitions to the Allies."[126]

Stimson's analysis was an interesting formulation intended to present Preparedness as a necessity not bound to one side or another. But he gave something away in his reference to Anglo-Saxon brotherhood. As he surely knew, while the Allies would have preferred for the United States to openly enter the war against Germany, they had good reason to appreciate the current American policy, which countenanced, if it did not encourage, Davison's program of massive financial and material aid to Britain and France. The Germans, as he accurately observed, found much to resent in American foreign policy.

At a meeting in New Rochelle in January 1916, Stimson laid out three essential components of an effective military force: an "ever ready, sea-going navy," an "adequate coast defense" and "a mobile army to be enlisted from the manhood of its citizens, with a regular force of about 200,000 men to be the brain and nucleus." In other words, a core regular army that could be drastically augmented by a national reserve trained under a universal military service law—much like Germany's.[127] To do otherwise, he warned, was to leave the country unprepared for eventual war, as it was during the War of 1812.

In an opinion piece that ran in the *New York Times* the following month, Stimson criticized proposals made in some quarters that called for strengthening the nation's military through an increase in the size of the National Guard. The Guard, he argued, could never be truly effective as long as it served "two masters": the states and the federal government. He also candidly described another defect involved in relying on an enlarged national guard system—the suspicion in which it was held by the "laboring classes." From the 1880s into the 1930s, states had commonly called out the National Guard to suppress pro-union labor agitation. Guardsmen, Stimson observed, were commonly seen as "representative[s] of capital being trained as a policeman against labor."[128] As long as that image persisted, it would be difficult to increase the military establishment by appealing to the large pool of citizenry beyond the middle and upper classes. Again, he proposed universal military training and creation of a large national reserve.

In addition to his efforts to promote Preparedness Camps and universal military training, Stimson took a small but practical step to ready local residents for military service. In December 1916, he helped form a rifle club for Huntington men and recruited some soldiers from Fort Totten near Bayside to provide some instruction.[129] Additionally, as an early supporter of Belgian relief, he made a personal pledge that Huntington would raise the funds to provide one thousand beds for Belgian children and saw to it that the drive was completed successfully.[130] As tireless as his Oyster Bay neighbor, Stimson was touring the more non-interventionist Midwest preaching the gospel of Preparedness when war was declared and his efforts, like the entire country, were radically transformed.[131]

With somewhat less fanfare, other Gold Coasters were advancing the cause of Preparedness. Trubee Davison, whose support for rearmament and intervention came naturally, took the initiative in recruiting his Yale classmates, primarily from the crew team, into a volunteer naval aviation squadron to be absorbed into the navy when the country entered the war. Inspired by the college-age flyers who made up the volunteer Lafayette Escadrille in France, Trubee set up a summer flying school for his classmates in the summer of 1916. The young men learned their craft on flying boats in nearby Port Washington, but their headquarters was the Davison estate at Peacock Point in Lattingtown.

His initial reservations overcome by Trubee's arguments, Harry Davison purchased Curtiss F-Boats for the fledgling group, which named itself the Yale Aero Coast Patrol Unit Number One.[132] Though the navy had provided some encouragement, it withheld official support or status to the fledgling aviators. Nevertheless, because there were so few such units available, the navy invited Yale Aero to take part in naval maneuvers in New York Harbor and along Long Island's South Shore in September 1916.

When the flyers returned to Yale that autumn, Trubee organized the Yale Aero Club with the goal of increasing the number of trained pilots for future navy use. After acquiring three more seaplanes with Harry's money, the Yale

The Yale Aero Squadron training at Port Washington, 1917. *Courtesy of the Library of Congress.*

The Yale Naval Air Reserve Squadron at Huntington Bay, 1918. *Author's collection.*

men began formalizing their relationship with the navy, leading to another name change—the First Yale Unit. It would not be long before their period of preparedness ended and their official enrollment as navy aviators began.

While the monied Old Westbury families were primarily devoted to equestrian pursuits, their North and South Shore counterparts were often yachtsmen, with many possessing vessels of considerable size. In November 1916, as Preparedness fever mounted, representatives of the major South Shore yachting clubs, including August Belmont Jr. and TR's uncle R.B. Roosevelt Jr., met at the Hotel Astor in Manhattan to organize the Volunteer Boat Association. The yachtsmen wished to organize themselves as a reserve for potential naval service but opposed a Naval Reserve bill then pending in Congress, as it would require them to enlist in the navy. Though they expressed their willingness to give their yachts to the government in times of war and undergo training during peace, "they will not enlist and place themselves at the beck and call of the Navy Department at all times."[133]

Naval officers present at the gathering responded that the yachtsmen would be a "valuable adjunct to the Navy," but they would require some training. As for their reservations, the navy officers suggested that the naval bill might be altered to meet some of their concerns.[134] The officers might well have smiled inwardly at the affluent yacht owners' belief that they could participate in a potential conflict, but only on their terms. In any event, once war was declared, many water-oriented members of the Gold Coast and elsewhere offered their yachts for naval service where they were deemed useful for antisubmarine operations.

Preparedness and interventionist enthusiasm—increasingly interchangeable—intensified as relations with Germany deteriorated. Typically, the monied classes on Long Island and elsewhere took the lead. In June 1916, they organized a weeklong fundraiser at Grand Central Palace in midtown Manhattan for various Allied relief organizations. Featuring a quasi–Middle Eastern theme, the Allied Bazaar was inaugurated by a society woman who rode horseback to the Palace's doors declaring the Bazaar ready for visitors. Fifty to sixty thousand people, including Robert Bacon, Anne Morgan, Mrs. Junius S. Morgan, the Russian ambassador and Ted Roosevelt's wife, Eleanor, attended the Bazaar during its one-week run. Inside, visitors found a variety of items, often high-end merchandise such as jewelry, tapestries and statuary, for sale. With advance ticket sales of $1 million, the Bazaar was deemed a great success.[135]

An even more opulent extravaganza was held in November, when New York society threw a costume-themed Ball of the Ten Allies at Madison Square Garden. Again, the event was intended as a fundraiser, with proceeds going to a number of Allied support groups, including the American Ambulance Corps serving in France, the British-American War Relief Fund, the Russian War Relief Fund and the French Heroes Fund, among others.[136] It also provided a stage for organizers and attendees to exhibit both their wealth as well as their convictions. Ball-goers were expected to arrive in costume, often symbolizing the Allied nations, and those who had neglected to secure an appropriate outfit could rent one at the Garden. The person wearing the most original costume was awarded a special prize: an automobile. Somewhere, Thorsten Veblen was smiling.

The ball commenced at nine o'clock with a cocktail hour, followed by dancing at ten. The evening took on a more serious tone at midnight, when a pageant celebrating the Allied nations began. After the singing of "The Star-Spangled Banner," prominent individuals symbolically garbed as Allied nations stepped to the front. While the New York and Long Island glitterati naturally predominated, the ball also attracted members of the upper crust from Boston, Philadelphia, Chicago and San Francisco. Vanderbilts, Morgans, Davisons, Fields, Ted and Eleanor Roosevelt and Huntington financial titan Otto Kahn were among the ball-goers.[137]

The *New York Times* reporters were dazzled—and starstruck—by the ball, describing it as "a gorgeous, glittering spectacle, eclipsing all other functions in New York for the benefit of war sufferers. It was as rich in color and as dazzling in jewels and costumes as a miniature of East Indian Durbar….It was also a big financial success."[138] The event also provided a dramatic display of the money and political power behind the pro-Allied interventionist movement. Their impatient campaign was shortly to bear fruit.

In May 1916, the National Guard was federalized, and members took oaths to both state and federal governments. The army was authorized to double its size over five years to 11,450 officers and 223,580 enlisted men. The National Guard expanded to 475,000 men who would be trained, equipped and paid by the federal government. Guardsmen would now take oaths of loyalty to both state and federal government and could be federalized in times of war and national crisis. Taking its cue from the student-dominated volunteer training camps, Reserve Officer Training Corps were greenlighted for adoption by colleges. Lastly, conscription was authorized for implementation in event of war.[139] All these measures were still in an embryonic state when the nation officially entered the struggle in 1917.

# CHAPTER 4

# MOBILIZING

*T*he Long Island elite had been among the most energetic and committed to Preparedness and what they deemed necessary intervention. Their recommendations, exhortations and denunciations were not empty bombast. Once the United States was officially at war with Germany, they walked the walk, throwing themselves into the war effort in numerous ways. Many of them, some above what was considered military age, joined one of the armed services. Others redoubled their efforts to expand and improve war industries. Still others, especially women, devoted themselves to vital support services, including the Red Cross, YWCA, soldier recreation rooms and military auxiliary units, such as the "Hello Girls," the young women who kept U.S. Army telephone communications running in France.

In early 1917, recognizing it could not withstand the combined weight of Allied power indefinitely, the German government and military high command adopted a plan to end the war, hopefully within a year. German forces would concentrate against the weakest of its major antagonists—Russia—and knock it out of the war. German troops in Russia would be transferred to the Western Front, where the heavily reinforced German army would launch massive offensives to force the Allies to conclude a peace on their terms. Simultaneously, they would unleash the U-boats in unrestricted submarine warfare to cut off supplies to Britain and France from their colonies and the United States. It was understood this would bring the United States into the war, but the German naval commanders convinced the Kaiser that it would take the United States months to fully prepare for war, and German submarines could prevent meaningful numbers of American troops from arriving in time to alter the balance on the battleground. It was a calculated risk. And it almost worked.

On February 3, the Wilson administration responded to the German resumption of unrestricted submarine warfare by severing diplomatic relations, widely understood as a preamble to war. All the pro-Allied and Preparedness organizations and leaders went into overdrive. At a meeting of New York University students in March 1917, Henry Stimson renewed his demands for universal military service. "If war comes," he exhorted the young men, "I shall regard it as the duty of this country to take a man's part, and to send troops to fight for what I believe to be the cause of free institutions on the battlefields of Europe."[140] Stimson dismissed the belief, popular in some quarters, that the American role in the war could be confined to naval operations as "very thoughtless."[141]

Like Roosevelt, Wood, Elihu Root and many others of his class and background, Stimson believed the American participation in the war would reap advantages beyond economic profits and international influence. As early as the 1890s, he had decided that a war "would be a wonderfully good thing for this country," reviving the energy, patriotism and sense of duty among the people. Moreover, the population at large would see its vitality restored and strengthened. The college-educated WASP elite would seize the opportunity to demonstrate its worth and right to lead through an ordeal by fire, what TR saw as being "blooded" like a fox hunter after his first successful chase.[142]

Stimson put the premise more obliquely at NYU, but his meaning was clear: the nation, and too many of its citizens, had grown soft, and the experience of war would redeem them from their decadent state. "We have been very rapidly becoming an indoor nation," he claimed. "One hundred years ago 90 percent of the people lived outdoors. More than a majority now live in cities. This is having an effect on the health and character that is not being offset. Physical benefits would be derived from military training."[143]

As expected, U-boat attacks on American and Allied ships mounted, and on April 2, Woodrow Wilson asked Congress for a declaration of war on Germany. Congress gave it to him four days later. A month later, Stimson and Roosevelt spoke at a gathering of one thousand, mostly students, at New York's Harvard Club. Their intention was to exhort the young Ivy Leaguers to sign up for the Reserve Officer Training Camps that had now replaced the Preparedness Camps. "Those who received unusual advantages," Roosevelt declared, "should pay the unusual reward" by serving as officers. Yelling at football games and such wasn't enough, the ex-president declared. "The men must prove their patriotism by service and sacrifice."[144] Stimson spoke next, warning his listeners that the War Department was not optimistic about the country's military readiness and was approaching war with Germany with "grim determination."[145]

The government had already announced plans to raise a mass army through means of conscription, and Roosevelt, returning to the podium, explained that the success of a large force of draftees "rested on the character of men who responded now for officer's camps."[146] In other words, the Doughboys—the First World War's "grunts"—would need the guiding hand and stolid leadership of the largely old-stock, collegiate elite. About three hundred men responded positively to Roosevelt and Stimson's presentation and signed up for the Reserve Officer camps following the meeting.[147]

After preaching Preparedness and duty for almost three years, Stimson felt he had an obligation to join the fight. It was not an easy task. He was a Republican, friend and ally of Theodore Roosevelt and nearly fifty years old—a résumé unlikely to impress the Wilson administration. Indeed, in his initial attempt to secure a commission, Stimson was bumped from a list of potential artillery officers by Secretary of War Newton Baker.

Undeterred, he arranged a face-to-face meeting with Baker to plead his case. The interview grew testy and, from the ex-secretary of war's perspective, went badly. Baker told him he did not intend to appoint "political" officers, as had been the case during the Civil War.[148] Exiting Baker's office, Stimson found the door of Major General Hugh Scott's office fortuitously—or deliberately—open. Scott, army chief of staff and an old friend, intervened and arranged for Stimson to join the Thirty-First Field Artillery currently training with the Seventy-Seventh Division at Camp Upton on eastern Long Island. He was given the rank of colonel.[149]

With war declared in April 1917, Trubee Davison and his fellows, dubbed "the Millionaires' Unit" by the press, departed for Palm Beach for more intensive official training. Harry Sr. picked up the costs of instruction.[150] The twenty-eight novice flyers returned to Long Island that June, making their headquarters at the Castle Edge estate overlooking Huntington Bay. The navy had provided the fledgling unit with two Curtiss N-seaplanes (pontoon versions of the famous JN-9 Jenny), while Gold Coast resident and financier Henry Payne Whitney supplied a Burgess-Dunne aircraft.[151]

The last bit of business before the Yale flyers were officially inducted into the navy as officers and pilots was their qualification flights scheduled

Davisons, Harry Jr., Harry and Trubee, at Peacock Point, 1918. *Courtesy of the Library of Congress.*

for July 28, 1917, at Huntington. It was a celebratory day replete with navy brass, throngs of spectators and family members crowding the shore or watching from boats in the bay. Twenty-seven of the twenty-eight members of the unit passed this last hurdle. Trubee, the founder and mainspring of the entire initiative, crashed his plane, broke his back and injured his spinal cord.[152] He spent six weeks in St. Luke's Hospital, where one of his well-wishers was TR. Unable to fly, and walking with difficulty, he remained in the navy on indeterminate shore duty. At home, he followed the war news from Europe, including the exploits of his Yale fellows, who joined the British in operations over the North Sea and Belgium. Among them were his younger brother Harry Jr. and classmates and neighbors Artemis Gates and Robert Jackson.

While Trubee and Harry Jr. were readying themselves and their classmates for navy aviation, Alice Davison, their sister, stepped up on behalf of the women in the area. She qualified as a wireless operator in 1916 and organized a women's wireless operators' unit for the Marconi company, which handled military communications. She later taught wireless at Hunter College, then a women's school, and became an inspector at one of the companies taken into government service.[153]

One prominent volunteer was not accepted for military service—former president Theodore Roosevelt. Since the summer of 1916 at least, Roosevelt had been laying plans to raise a division of volunteers on the line of his Spanish-American War Rough Riders.[154] To press his case, TR swallowed his pride and sought a meeting with Woodrow Wilson, the man at whom he had spat venom for two years. Wilson listened respectfully but made no commitments when Roosevelt called at the White House on April 9, 1917.

But the consensus among the professional military men—Chief of Staff Tasker Bliss and General John J. Pershing, newly appointed commander of the American Expeditionary Forces (AEF)—was negative. Wilson likely felt a certain amount of satisfaction when he rejected Roosevelt's request via telegram on May 18. After stating he would wish to pay both TR and the Allies the "compliment" of allowing the ex-president to lead his volunteers alongside the Allied armies, he added, "This is not the time for compliments, or any action not calculated to contribute to the ultimate success of the war. The business now at hand is undramatic, practical and of scientific definiteness and precision."[155]

Roosevelt would have to experience the Great War vicariously through his sons. His ally and friend General Leonard Wood, long a thorn in the side of Wilson, was likewise denied any active role in the American war effort.

On hearing that Pershing was preparing to sail for France with an initial—and small—contingent of U.S. troops, Roosevelt, who had jumped him in rank during his presidency, contacted the AEF commander and asked that Ted and Archie be allowed to serve in this advance detachment as privates if necessary. Pershing accepted the young Roosevelts into his embryonic First Division, but with ranks more commensurate with those they had earned at Plattsburgh. Ted was appointed major, in charge of a battalion, and Archie a first lieutenant. Quentin entered the U.S. Army Air Service, and Kermit, after a brief stint at Plattsburgh, now an officer candidate school, made use of his father's connections to get in the British army and embarked for Mesopotamia (modern-day Iraq.)

Eleanor, Ted's wife, threw herself into the war effort as energetically as she had the cause of Preparedness. Through her acquaintance with General J. Franklin Bell, who headed the embarkation department in New York (he would later command at Camp Upton in Suffolk County), Eleanor arranged for her two brothers to sail on the first transports for France. The entire

Roosevelt family was on hand to see them off. An excited and probably overwrought TR injected a sense of unease at the parting by saying, apparently approvingly, that he expected at least one of his sons to be wounded, perhaps killed, in glorious battle.[156] Later, thinking better of his words, he wrote Archie—twice—that once he had seen combat and proven himself and was then "offered a staff place *in which you can be useful*, it would then be foolish to refuse it, merely because it was less dangerous."[157] He expressed similar feelings to Ted.

Meanwhile, Eleanor, who had enlisted as a YMCA volunteer, learned that the government was preparing to announce a prohibition on soldiers' wives sailing for Europe and the war zones. She quickly applied to the YMCA, one of the organizations providing recreational support for the troops, for a position as a full-time overseas volunteer. Her request was granted, and she left for France on July 2, 1917, beating the government's order. She was appointed head of all women volunteers in France and was headquartered in Paris, where she lived in the house of an absent aunt.[158] Her abode became the central meeting place for the members of the Roosevelt clan whenever they were able to visit Paris.

Dr. Richard Derby, who not only married a Roosevelt but was absorbed by them, had trained at Plattsburgh along with his brothers-in-law. He entered the army at the same time as Ted and Archie but followed a different trajectory. While in basic training at Fort Oglethorpe in Georgia, Derby sent a letter to the *New York Times* chastising the younger cohort of doctors for not flocking to the colors. He reported encountering few young men in the medical corps and estimated the average age of army doctors as just under forty.[159] He castigated younger doctors seeking safe and comfortable postings at base hospitals, assignments that he argued would be better accomplished by the older medical men, allowing the younger ones to employ their skills and stamina near the front.[160] While not stating so directly, Derby was charging the younger cohort of physicians as "slackers," those who were not pulling their full weight in the war effort—a potent criticism in 1917–18. Sounding a bit like his father-in-law, Derby closed his letter with an appeal to patriotism: "Will you younger men make it necessary for the Government to draft you into the service? What reason will you someday give to your children for not having answered the call of your country in its hour of need."[161]

After completing basic training at Camp Oglethorpe, Derby attended an accelerated officer training program run by the French at Harvard.[162] Following his commission as a major in the medical reserve, he spent

September and October 1917 at Camp Upton in eastern Long Island. Derby, whose brother Lloyd was also posted to Upton, took advantage of proximity to Sagamore Hill to visit his father-in-law and vent his frustrations about shortages of weapons, cold weather gear and slack training. Humiliated by Wilson, TR had reverted to his earlier role as one of the administration's most caustic critics and used information obtained from Derby in his broadsides against the administration, condemning it for failure to prepare for war and then proving incompetent in running it. In October, Derby was sent to Chickamauga in northern Georgia, where he was appointed assistant divisional surgeon in the Second Division, which shipped out for France on November 12, 1917.[163]

Quentin, the youngest of TR's sons, joined the Army Air Service in the spring of 1917. Inheriting his father's weak eyes, he memorized the eye chart so he could pass the required physical. Conveniently stationed at Hazelhurst Field in Mineola, he commuted back and forth from Sagamore Hill, sleeping in his boyhood home while training at the base.

With two airfields, Hazelhurst and Mitchel, and Camp Mills, the nearby army training facility, the Mineola–Garden City area resembled a small military city. The selection of the Mineola hub for flying fields and army camps was determined by the topography of central Nassau—the Hempstead Plains. Flat, still largely agricultural and undeveloped, they were well suited for military encampments and aerodromes.

The bases were also in easy traveling distance of Old Westbury on the southern edge of the Gold Coast, an upscale enclave of socially prominent, politically connected one-percenters. Among these were Henry Payne Whitney and his wife, Gertrude Vanderbilt Whitney, longtime financial backers of pro-Allied and Preparedness initiatives including the Ambulance Americaine. Quentin began courting their eldest daughter, Flora "Foufie" Whitney, and proposed to her in May 1917. Both families were initially wary of the match. The Whitneys considered TR a loose cannon, and TR viewed them as idle plutocrats. Plutocrats they might have been, but they were accomplished in their own right. Henry was a naturalist as well as a sportsman, and Gertrude was a sculptor and artist who later founded the Whitney Museum of Art in New York City. Flora's charm won TR over, and the Whitneys came to accept Quentin before he sailed for France on July 23, 1917.

Trubee Davison later declared that "no branch of military service had a greater appeal for the young American than did the air service."[164] Old Westbury families seemed especially drawn to the new, exciting field of aviation. John S. "Jay" Phipps, whose home, Westbury House, was and

Quentin Roosevelt and Flora Whitney, 1917. *Courtesy of Sagamore Hill National Historic Site, National Park Service, Oyster Bay, New York.*

remains one of Long Island's architectural jewels, joined the Army Air Service despite the relatively advanced age of forty-three. There was no question of him being posted to enlisted ranks. After some training at Plattsburgh, he was commissioned a captain and stationed in Texas before transfer to Mineola, a short drive from Old Westbury. Phipps lived at home, his military service taking on the character of a day job. He enjoyed playing the gracious host and inviting fellow officers to Westbury House for lunch.[165]

Master of Westbury House. Jay Phipps as an Army Air Service major, 1918. *Courtesy of the Collections of Old Westbury Gardens.*

Near neighbors of Phipps, the Hitchcocks of Broad Hollow Farm played a more active and energetic role in the nation's young air forces. Like many, if not most, of the community's families, Thomas Hitchcock and his son, Thomas Jr. or Tommy, were noted equestrians and polo players, active in the local social and club life, including the prestigious Meadowbrook Polo Club. Thomas Sr. (1860–1941) was one of the founders of the famed club, an initiative that was joined by other luminaries such as August Belmont. The senior Hitchcock had also helped make Aiken, South Carolina, a center of horse-related sports and began spending most winters in the upcountry area. When Vanderbilts and Whitneys also alighted there during the colder months, Aiken effectively became the southern satellite of Long Island polo/equestrians.

The Hitchcocks instinctively identified with the Allied cause. Thomas Sr.'s Anglo-Saxon heritage was likely deepened by the time he spent at Brasenose College at Oxford University, where his father had sent him for his higher education. He was introduced to polo at Oxford and played alongside well-heeled British aristocrats including Douglas Haig, commander of the British army on the Western Front in 1917–18. Tradition, education and

Tommy Hitchcock and Flora Whitney, Meadowbrook Polo Club, 1912. *Courtesy of the Library of Congress.*

life experience combined to foster an Anglo-Saxon-based American identity that promoted a view of the war from a perspective of a perceived joint Anglo-American interest.

Thomas Jr.—Tommy—attempted to join the air service when the United States entered the conflict, but at only seventeen, he was rejected as too young. Refusing to be put off, he managed to get into the French Air Force with a little help from a neighbor acquaintance, the ex-president in Oyster Bay. His father, the senior Thomas, also wanted to play his part and showed his solidarity with his son by enlisting in the air service even though he was over fifty. At the time of his discharge, he was believed to be the oldest member of the flying services.[166]

Although at the opposite end of the age spectrum, Thomas Sr. learned to fly at Mineola and was commissioned a major. Apparently, he was considered accomplished enough in the air that he was put in charge of instruction at Hazelhurst. Reportedly, he never went a day without flying.[167] Jay Phipps, also older than most members of the Army Air Service, remained stateside during the war. He ended his career at Hazelhurst serving as chief executive officer under his neighbor, Hitchcock. Thomas

Sr.'s daughter followed family tradition and worked the counter at the Red Cross convalescent house on the base.[168]

Not all Old Westbury residents looked to the sky for their service. Already a member of the old line "silk stocking" Seventh Regiment New York National Guard, Bradley Martin, husband of Jay Phipps's sister, Helen, stayed with the infantry. Martin, who named his estate Knole, descended from a family of bankers and merchants. His parents were noted New York socialites well remembered for their 1897 Louis XV costume ball at the Waldorf-Astoria. Costing a reputed $180,000, it was deemed "the most ostentatious in United States history."[169]

Martin (1873–1963) lived a more subdued lifestyle by Gold Coast standards but was as eager to join the new American crusade as his fellows. Leaving the National Guard, he attended the Officer Training Camp at Plattsburgh in May 1917 and was commissioned an infantry major the following August. He was then assigned to the 3rd Battalion, 308th Infantry Regiment, which was part of the newly created 77th Division training at Camp Upton.

Martin's wife, Helen, though totally supportive of her husband's decisions, could not suppress the feelings of anxiety that many felt as their loved ones prepared to leave for the battlefields of Europe. When Helen arrived at Plattsburgh in August 1917 to witness Bradley's graduation from Officer Training School, he told her he had just been assigned to the infantry. Helen had mixed feelings and wrote her father confessing, "I am happy for Bradley's sake and very proud of him. But my courage fails me when I think that sometime this winter he will leave for the front. In my heart I hoped he would be in the Quartermaster Department and at least escape being in the terrible trenches."[170] Such was not to be.

Camp Upton, named for Civil War general Emory Upton, was one of seventeen entirely new training centers created expressly for the "National Army"'—formed from the draftee divisions. Gouged out of the Long Island pine barrens in eastern Suffolk County, the facility was ready to begin receiving the newly inducted men when Martin was posted there in early September 1917. Composed primarily of men from the New York City area, the Seventy-Seventh Division was also known as the Metropolitan or Melting Pot division due to the large number of immigrants and first-generation members. The division proudly embraced its New York character by taking the Statue of Liberty as its insignia.

The army soon found it had to deal with many languages and religions and ultimately handled the challenge reasonably well. It was aided by several support organizations such as the YMCA, Knights of Columbus and Jewish War Council, which established facilities at Upton and the other military camps to provide leisure activities and moral and ethno-religious support. Upton even provided kosher food for its Orthodox Jewish troops.[171] The hopes TR held that the Preparedness Camps would foster democracy and national spirit by bringing men from diverse backgrounds together foundered on the reality of their elite Waspishness. It was in the training camps of the Great War that a genuine sense of national identity—what some might call Americanism—was at least to some degree forged. For Martin and Dick Derby, who was briefly stationed at Upton, the experience must have been educational.

The great exception to the melting pot experience of the war was race. The army maintained the practice of racial segregation it had followed since the Civil War. While African American troops trained at Camp Upton and elsewhere, they were organized in all-black units and quartered in separate barracks.

Not surprisingly, the Long Island elite were well represented in naval service, either through personal service or the donation of their large steam yachts, which were in demand as patrol boats and submarine chasers. Among these was Scottish-born Robert E. Tod, owner of the 150-acre estate Thistleton in Syosset. Tod immigrated to the United States in 1883 and joined a family-owned banking house in Indiana, where he prospered through finance and investment in property and railroads. Like many successful Midwesterners, he was attracted to the lifestyle of the eastern luminaries and relocated to Long Island after retiring from banking in 1913. Though he also enjoyed the horse and hunting scene—Thistleton was home to the Meadowbrook Hounds for many years—his real passion was yachting. He was a member of several yacht clubs, including the elite New York Yacht Club, where he served as commodore.

There was little doubt where his sympathies lay regarding the war, and despite his relatively advanced age of fifty, he enlisted in the navy on March 6, 1917, as war with Germany loomed. Nor was that the extent of his support for his adopted country's war effort. Seeing the need for small, fast vessels to combat the U-boat threat, he joined Harold Vanderbilt, Alfred I. DuPont and Payne Whitney in funding "a flotilla of submarine chasers which will," in the gushing words of the *New York Times*, "surpass in fighting efficiency any vessel of their design since the great war began."[172]

Given the rank of provisional lieutenant, his first assignment was aboard the yacht *Corsair*, which Jack Morgan had lent to the navy. Tod was third ranking officer and chief navigation officer. In early 1918, the *Corsair* sailed

Robert E. Tod, circa 1918.
*Courtesy of the Library of Congress.*

for France, where Tod was transferred to shore duty and where he would make his most significant contributions to the Allied cause.

Also onboard the *Corsair* was a junior officer who combined both yachting experience with an intimate knowledge of the vessel—Junius Spencer Morgan III. Junius had grown up on the family's estate, Matinecock Point, and, like most of the North Shore families, was introduced to sailing at an early age. He learned about motor vessels on his father's and grandfather's yachts. After the war, he built his own estate, Salutations, on the opposite end of the East Island from his father's home.

Pro-Allied and pro-Preparedness, Junius had visited the war zones in France as early as 1915. He became a member of the Naval Militia, the naval equivalent of the National Guard, and participated in maneuvers held off Montauk in August 1916.[173] Junius was also a founding member of the Power Craft Association of the Third Naval District, New York, whose major purpose was to provide motorized yachts and similar vessels for coastal defense in time of war. Upon the American entry into the conflict, Junius volunteered for active duty and was sent to the Naval Reserve Officers' Training School, the navy's version of the Army Officer Training School, for a ten-week course. Commissioned an ensign, he found

*Above*: The Morgan power yacht *Corsair. Courtesy of the Glen Cove Public Library Robert R. Coles Long Island History Room.*

*Left*: Junius Morgan (*center*), 1917. *Courtesy of the Library of Congress.*

himself assigned to a familiar vessel, his father's *Corsair*, on which Robert Tod was already serving.[174]

Morgans, Davisons, Hitchcocks, Bacons, Bradleys, Derbys, Roosevelts, Stimsons and younger Stettiniuses were all in uniform or actively supporting the war effort by the close of 1917. Those who had hoped and agitated for the United States to enter the conflict were soon to experience it firsthand.

# CHAPTER 5

# THE WAR AT HOME

*I*n the first months following the United States' entry into the war, many feared attacks from German saboteurs or U-boats, and a few even watched anxiously for a German invasion. With young men joining the army or being drafted, concern about German activities (that never materialized) merged with widespread anxiety regarding radical labor agitation to cause many localities to create local Home Guards.

Home Guards were drawn from the ranks of men exempted from the draft or above draft age. They wore army-style uniforms and carried rifles, often obsolete models such as the Spanish-American War–issued Krag-Jorgensens. As neither violent strikes nor German raiders appeared by the end of 1917, they became primarily involved with social activities and parading at patriotic rallies such as those connected with Liberty Loan sales. The Liberty Loans—four launched during the war and one renamed a Victory Loan afterward—were the government's primary method of funding the conflict, and citizens of all classes were exhorted to purchase them.

Equestrian pursuits were a major passion among Long Island's Gold Coast/Old Westbury set, and in May 1917, some of the more prominent families drew on it in launching their own version of the Home Guard, which was titled the Westbury Reserve No. 3. The unit was founded by twenty-six members of the exclusive Meadowbrook and Piping Rock Clubs, "among whom are some of the best-known polo players and cross-country riders in the East."[175] Prominent among the Reserve's members were Robert Bacon, and J.P. and W. Russell Grace. Grace also offered his estate in Old Westbury for use as a rifle range.[176] All members were appointed deputy sheriffs and authorized to carry pistols. Not to be left behind, twelve women members of the Piping Rock Club formed a Red Cross unit and enlisted for first aid work if wartime events required it.[177] Their services were never needed.

While the Home Guards often turned out at public events, they were occasionally called upon for more specialized tasks. Among these was providing security at the 1917 wedding of Frances Tracey Morgan, daughter of J.P. Morgan Jr. and sister of Junius. Probably mindful of the assassination attempt on Jack in 1915, and fearful of another such attempt on the family, the Glen Cove Home Guards were detailed to St. John's Church of Lattingtown, where the ceremony took place. The church, established by J.P. Morgan, was cordoned off by motorcycle police and the Glen Cove Guards with instructions "to keep strangers away."[178] Further security was provided at the causeway entrance to East Island, where the reception was held, and some observers took note of "a small squadron of seaplanes and flying boats [that] circled over Long Island Sound."[179] With Morgans, Davisons and their compatriots gathered for the event, an attack by German agents would have delivered a powerful symbolic as well as material blow to the burgeoning American war effort. But no such attempt materialized.

Long Island's high-profile families lent their names, their talents and their wallets to a wide variety of events and causes supporting the war effort. The most highly touted and successful fundraiser of 1917, both socially and financially, was the Rosemary Farm Red Cross Pageant hosted by Roland Ray Conklin on his Lloyd Harbor estate.

Conklin was descended from a branch of an old Huntington family that had joined the great American trek westward in the nineteenth century. Born in 1858 in Illinois, he made his fortune in Kansas City real estate

before relocating to New York in 1893. There he organized the North American Trust Company and was appointed fiscal agent for the United States government in Cuba. Returning to his ancestral roots, in 1907 he purchased a plot of land in Lloyd Harbor a little north of Huntington village. Situated on a prime piece of sloping uplands, his new estate, which he named Rosemary Farm after his daughter, offered exceptional vistas of Cold Spring Harbor and Oyster Bay to the west and Long Island Sound to the northwest. Theodore Roosevelt's Sagamore Hill lay just across Cold Spring Harbor on Cove Neck (now Oyster Bay Cove).

Though the mansion (burned in 1990) was impressive, the most unique aspect of Rosemary Farm was an outdoor amphitheater laid out on a stretch of property where the land descended gradually from the house to the water. The initiative for the amphitheater apparently came from Conklin's wife, Mary McFadden, a former opera singer, who wished to create a showplace for musicians, singers and poets. Spectators would sit on the terraces that sloped down to a small moat-like stretch of water that separated them from performers who stood on a spur of land on the opposite bank. Up to four thousand people could be accommodated for a performance.[180]

In September 1917, working with a group of theatrical producers, actors and Red Cross officials, Conklin offered the farm and amphitheater to the Red Cross for an elaborate, star-studded fundraiser. The theater people, actors and producers, donated their time and talents, while costs were borne by an array of the most prominent members of society on Long Island, New York and, in some cases, beyond. Numbered among the patrons were Major and Mrs. Robert Bacon, Mr. and Mrs. August Belmont, Harry and Kate Davison, Mrs. E.H. Harriman, Judge and Mrs. Robert Lovett, Harvard president A.L. Lowell and his wife, Clarence Mackay, Mr. and Mrs. Emlen

Rosemary Farm, Lloyd Harbor, circa 1917. *Courtesy of the Huntington Historical Society.*

Program, Rosemary Farm Red Cross Pageant, 1917. *Courtesy of the Huntington Historical Society.*

Roosevelt, Mr. and Mrs. Elihu Root, Edward Stettinius and his wife, Colonel and Mrs. Henry Stimson, Louis Comfort Tiffany and his spouse and, of course, Roland and Mary Conklin.

The pageant was divided into two acts. The first featured a series of vignettes in which actors performed allegorical or historical portrayals symbolic of the key Allied nations. For example, France was represented by a short scene drawn from the life of Joan of Arc and England by a representation of the court of Elizabeth I. In the second phase, "The Drawing of the Sword," actors representing the Allied nations proclaimed their justifications for entering the Great War. One hundred actors, including some of the most popular thespians of the day, several of whom would enjoy careers spanning several decades, appeared in the pageant. Among these were John and Ethel Barrymore, Jeanne Eagles and Peggy Wood. John Philip Sousa and a navy band augmented the music, and the entire event was filmed for further distribution.[181]

Rehearsals for the pageant were held through September, almost up to the day of performance on October 5. Special motor transportation was arranged to convey attendees from Huntington's Long Island Rail Road station to Rosemary Farm. The Red Cross Pageant was a smashing success on all levels. Huntington's local paper, the *Long Islander*, was jubilant, gushing that the pageant was "the finest affair of its kind ever produced in the country....It put Huntington on the map, not only for that day, but for days of advertising of the event in the big metropolitan dailies....Never before has there been such an aggregation of leading actors of the country at a single event."[182] Nor was this simply local boosterism. *Vogue* magazine described it as "a most gorgeous pageant, which proved to be at the same time the most successful of war benefits."[183] The event itself raised $50,000, with much more projected from distribution of the film.[184]

The Rosemary Farm Red Cross Pageant might have boasted the most star power, but it was not the only high-profile wartime fundraiser organized by Long Island's leading families. One of 1918's most elaborate war charity events, the highlight of the summer season for the Long Island glitterati, was the Gymkhana held on Jay Phipps's estate in Old Westbury. The Gymkhana, a frolicsome equestrian event of Indian origin, was intended as a fundraiser for the British and Patriotic Fund, which provided support to wives and families of Canadian and British troops, including those who had enlisted in the United States.[185] Harry P. Davison, then head of the American Red Cross, gave the event his blessing. Tickets sold for five dollars, and attendees could also try their luck in raffles for war

*Above*: Edward Ireland as La Hire, French episode, Rosemary Farm Red Cross Pageant, 1917. *Courtesy of the Huntington Historical Society.*

*Opposite*: Jeanne Eagles as Jeanne de Clairmont, French episode, Rosemary Farm Red Cross Pageant, 1917. *Courtesy of the Huntington Historical Society.*

relics, pony rides and a flight in an Italian Caproni bomber that flew over from Hazelhurst Field for the festivities.

After a week's postponement due to bad weather, the Gymkhana opened on June 29, 1918. Soldiers, mostly officers of the various Allied countries, mixed with the crowds generously sprinkled with members of New York and Long Island society. Attendees included Whitneys, Belmonts,

The Gymkhana. Westbury House, Old Westbury, 1918. *Courtesy of the Library of Congress.*

The Gymkhana. Westbury House, Old Westbury, 1918. *Courtesy of the Library of Congress.*

Mackays, Bacons, Graces and Hitchcocks, plus, of course, the members of the Phipps family.

The early afternoon was dominated by aerial displays performed by flyers from the Mineola air bases. Then the horse-and-rider events began. These included races and a mounted tug of war in which members of the Allied military forces participated. The Americans triumphed in that event.[186] More lighthearted heats included the Gretna Green, in which a couple rode on separate horses to a table while holding hands, dismounted, wrote their names in a book, remounted and rode back to their starting place, hands still clasped. Another competition required competitors to saddle up, ride a certain distance, dismount, light a cigar, remount and ride a farther distance, dismount, drink a bottle of soda, ride again to another area to dismount, put on a night shirt, open a parasol and then ride back to the finish. There was also a pig-sticking competition, although a live pig was replaced by a ball to spare the audience the sight and sounds of a squealing, dying, bloody animal. The event was deemed a success, netting $10,000 for the fund.[187]

Interestingly, while the Gymkhana was going on in Old Westbury, a fundraiser for the benefit of a different Allied nation was taking place to the north in Glen Cove on the estate of Mr. and Mrs. George DuPont Pratt. The "garden fete" was organized in support of the Italian War Relief Fund of America, and it featured Italian members of the Metropolitan Opera Company, recitations and dancing exhibitions by students of Isadora Duncan.[188] Unsurprisingly, the Gymkhana was a more popular draw.

High-profile, celebrity-laden spectacles were only part of the North Shore's war effort. Residents also lent the weight of their prominence and position to more mundane, but essential, measures. As the United States entered and geared up for the war, the question of food supply, among other strategic materials, caused anxiety in both the government and public at large. The United States had been exporting massive amounts of food to the western Allies during the 1914–17 period. Now it had to maintain those shipments, both for Allied troops and civilian refugees, and it also needed to feed its own troops, as well as the American civilian population.

To expand and expedite the food production, the federal government created the Food Administration, run by the young problem solver Herbert Hoover, who had headed the Commission for Relief in Belgium. Hoover decided against rationing (adopted in the Great War's sequel) and relied instead on voluntary conservation and expanded production. The public was urged to practice "meatless" and "wheatless" days and encouraged to increase the consumption of corn, fish and pork in lieu of wheat and

Westbury House, probably July 4, 1918. Children symbolically attired to represent the Allied nations. *Courtesy of Old Westbury Gardens.*

beef. To implement the program, both homeowners and food merchants took a pledge to use substitutions and not sell itemized foodstuffs on certain days. Compliance was largely obtained through social coercion. Despite a preference for citizen compliance, the Food Administration could, and sometimes did, shut down a bakery or butcher shop for short periods as a punishment.

With its extensive agricultural sector, Long Island farmers increased the acreage under production and turned to high school students, Boy Scouts and sometimes young women as substitutes for the young farm workers drafted into the armed forces.

The upper echelons were not directly involved in production, but as the nation embraced the cause of food conservation, they undertook symbolic, often well publicized measures to increase the national larder. Many estates began laying out Liberty Gardens, vegetable plots of varying size that signaled their participation in the cause. Among those whose measures in this regard were applauded by the media were the Davisons of Peacock Point. In what a later age would dub a "puff piece," an August 1918 article in the *New Country Life* extolled the Davisons as a "100 percent war family."[189] The article concentrated on Davison's conversion of much of his Peacock Point estate to food production. In addition to fruits and vegetables, the polo field was turned over to ten Jersey cows for grazing, while a corn crop was dedicated to providing feed for chickens.

Davison's intention was not commercial, as little if any of his produce would make itself to markets. The idea was to set a public example in self-sufficiency and, however tangentially, reduce the demand on the open market, thus freeing more American food for the war effort. Likewise, Davison reduced his estate's workforce, ostensibly freeing up more men for military service and war work.[190] While Davison's contributions were necessarily marginal, they served as a public display of personal commitment to the national crusade, promoting a "we're all in this together" ethos.

Davison was not alone. Mrs. Winslow S. Pierce grew a "large crop of potatoes in her war garden at Dunstable, her country estate in Bayville."[191] She offered her crop only to Bayville residents at a lower price than market.[192] Roland R. Conklin, who had hosted the celebrated Rosemary Farm Red Cross Pageant, reportedly turned every tillable acre on his four-hundred-acre Lloyd Harbor estate to the production of potatoes and onions for the 1917 growing season.[193] Mrs. Jay Phipps joined with Mrs. Emlen Roosevelt in promoting the consumption of fish on "meatless" days.[194] Meanwhile, the youngest of Jay Phipps's daughters, Peggy, took up work at the Hicksville Canning Kitchen, where she was described as a "champion bean stringer and bean cutter."[195]

Such undertakings by the wealthy and prominent on Long Island and elsewhere throughout the nation had a negligible effect on American food production, which covered all its demands primarily through the astounding productivity of the nation's commercial farmers. Nevertheless, the estate Liberty Gardens and volunteerism, at home as well as in the service, signaled their commitment to and participation in the nation's crusade to "make the world safe for democracy."

Beyond the gesture, some prominent Gold Coast families performed signal roles outside the armed forces. Harry Davison, whose efforts to fund and arm the Allies set the country on a course that led to open warfare with Germany, became one of the Wilson administration's "Dollar a Day men." These men were industrialists and bankers whose expertise was tapped by the government to ensure the efficient operation of American industry and transportation, necessary to a successful national war effort.

To ensure production and eliminate bottlenecks, Bernard Baruch took the helm at the War Industries Board, Hoover oversaw the Food Administration and the nation's railroads were effectively nationalized under the Railway Administration. All the leading members of these wartime agencies served voluntarily at the symbolic wage of a dollar a day.

Though ordinarily distrustful of "Wall Street men," Woodrow Wilson was brought around to the idea that Davison was the right man to head the Red Cross War Council.[196] The Red Cross War Council's tasks included providing volunteers to aid the sick and wounded of the war, supplying relief in war-devastated zones and providing communications between the armed forces and the public. The Red Cross was also credited with playing a key role in keeping France and Italy in the war during the grim months of 1917 and early 1918.[197]

As Russia was convulsed by revolution in 1917, Davison and Lamont organized and funded a mission to the tottering ally in an attempt to keep it in the war. Even after the Bolsheviks (communists) seized power in November 1917 and began negotiating peace with Germany, Davison persisted in the fanciful hope that Russia could be brought back into the struggle.[198] The war was over when Davison finally abandoned any hope for dealing with the Bolshevik government.[199]

Whether in Washington, at home or abroad, Davison, given the honorary rank of major general, took on his assignment with the same energy and effectiveness with which he had run the Morgan Bank. His initial effort was to raise $100 million for the Red Cross by means of the Kick the Kaiser Campaign, a number many believed well nigh impossible to achieve. Over $113 million was raised during the first week.[200] Rallies, membership drives and patriotic fervor resulted in two million adults and eleven million young people signing up for Red Cross work.

Under Davison's leadership, the Red Cross raised $400 million by November 1918.[201] Edward House, Wilson's confidential advisor and *eminence gris*, considered Davison's leadership of the Red Cross War Council as "perhaps the finest piece of executive management accomplished during the entire war."[202] The government publicly recognized his achievements by awarding him the Distinguished Service Medal. For her part, Harry's wife, Kate Trubee Davison, took on the position of treasurer of the War Work Council of the National Board of the Young Women's Christian Association (YWCA). The council provided lodging and recreational activities for young women seeking war work at military bases or at munitions and weaponry plants.

She was not alone in her service. Overseas, another prominent society woman, Mrs. William K. Vanderbilt, acted as a liaison between the U.S. and

Alice Davison and Flora Whitney, Red Cross Parade, 1918. *Courtesy of the Library of Congress.*

*Above*: Harry Davison greeting African American soldiers, Winchester, England, 1918. *Courtesy of the Library of Congress.*

*Right*: Harry Davison Jr., 1918. *Courtesy of the Library of Congress.*

French Red Cross and ran the canteen (food) department. Indeed, while the leadership of the Red Cross was dominated by men, women made up the majority of volunteers. "Without the women, there could be no Red Cross," Harry declared.[203]

Davison journeyed to Europe in early 1918, getting firsthand knowledge of the situation in Britain, France and Belgium. High-level meetings with American and Allied officials alternated with visits to hospitals and refugee centers in the war zones. On a second trip to Europe in the summer of 1918, he found the time to visit with his son Harry Jr., who was serving in a naval aviation unit near Dunkirk. All the time, he was preparing the funding drives necessary for the Red Cross to do its work.

The leading North Shore families played conspicuous roles in providing the financial and morale resources necessary to put the nation on a wartime footing. While many gave themselves enthusiastically to such measures as Liberty Loan and Red Cross drives, recreation and support facilities for soldiers and sailors and such, others were serving their country face-to-face with the enemy on the front lines.

# CHAPTER 6

# OVER THERE

*T*he Gold Coast/Old Westbury families who had proven their commitment to the Allies in both word and deed embraced Wilson's call to arms enthusiastically. Those above military age commonly served in noncombatant roles, as was the case with Harry Davison and his work with the Red Cross. Others played a conspicuous part in the sale of Liberty Bonds, the government's major way of raising funds to cover wartime spending. A number of this older cohort entered military service in administrative roles, as did Thomas Hitchcock Sr. and Jay Phipps. But most of the younger generation, and some whose years might have kept them out of the front lines, put their civilian lives on hold and joined the crusade they had done so much to ignite.

The Colonel, as Theodore Roosevelt preferred to be called post-presidency, might have been frustrated and disappointed by being blocked from an active role in the war, but he supported it with all the energy his declining health would allow. Having watched his sons and one daughter-in-law sail for France, he remained eagle-eyed in his vigilance over the Wilson administration's wartime performance and pounced on any perceived deficiency. His writing and speaking schedule scarcely showed any sign of flagging, and he remained visible and politically potent through his appearances at Liberty Bond rallies and visitations to military camps.

TR visited Camp Upton on November 23, 1917, admonishing the young draftees to reject the arguments of pacifists whom he thought undercut the war effort and lacked the required quotient of American manliness. In

August 1918, as the American Expeditionary Forces were coming into their own on the French battlefields, Roosevelt received a delegation of twenty soldiers from Camp Mills on the Hempstead Plains. He gave them a tour of Sagamore Hill's North Room, where mementoes of his hunts, political and military careers were displayed. Perhaps resting his eyes on his sword and hat from the Rough Rider days, he told the new generation of warriors that "the war with Spain was a small one compared to the one you boys are going to participate in, but the boys in it had the stuff in them, just as I am sure you fellows have. I am certain you boys will make good. I wish I were going over with you. If you happen to run across my boys give them my love."[204] TR's boys were already fulfilling their father's hopes, and one would lose his life in the process.

The former president also gave generously to organizations supporting the war effort. While his income was not in the rarefied elevations of his prospective in-laws, the Whitneys, he received $25,000 a week writing for newspapers and an additional $5,000 a year for his articles in the *Metropolitan* (all in current dollars). He still had some inheritance from his father, plus the $45,482.83 from the Nobel Peace Prize award he had received for mediating an end to the Russo-Japanese War in 1905.[205] Among those who benefited from his largesse were the Red Cross, Japanese Red Cross, International Red Cross, Australian Red Cross, Jewish Welfare Board, YMCA Negro Division and Belgian War Refugees, as well as donations he sent to families of wounded Allied soldiers.[206] All in all, it was a varied selection of charities and one that reflected his own understanding of the nation and the world war.

Meanwhile, Ted and Archie were in France with the First Division receiving advanced training in modern, industrialized warfare from the French. Dick Derby would arrive with the Second Division a little later in the fall, while Kermit, wishing to avoid another stint in training, had joined the British army and was serving in Mesopotamia. Quentin spent the summer mastering flying at Hazelhurst Field while courting Flora in his off hours.

The First and Second Divisions, soon followed by the Forty-Second, which trained at Camp Mills, and the Twenty-Sixth "Yankee Division" formed from New England National Guard units, were initially posted in "quiet" sectors on the Western Front where they received advanced instruction in the realities of combat from the French. This set the template for all U.S. units that followed as soon as they completed basic training in America.

Eleanor's house on the edge of the Bois de Boulogne served as Roosevelt Central in Paris, with all the Roosevelt boys and their friends staying with

Roosevelts in France. *Left to right*: Richard Derby, Eleanor Roosevelt, Kermit Roosevelt, Archie Roosevelt (*sitting*). *Courtesy of Sagamore Hill National Historic Site, National Park Service, Oyster Bay, New York.*

her when they could. Clean beds and good food were an attraction, but the opportunity to see family loomed even larger. Rank had its privileges, and the Roosevelts received their mail from the Paris branch of the Farmer's Loan and Trust Company, where cousin Oliver Roosevelt worked. It was faster than army mail. Flora wrote Quentin through contacts at the Morgan Bank's Paris office for the same reason.[207]

Though the American Expeditionary Forces did not become involved in major operations until June, some units saw action in small operations, raids and counterraids. In early March 1918, Archie became the first of the Roosevelts to be wounded in just such a contest. At about 5:00 a.m., he was hit by shrapnel that severed the nerves above the elbow and mangled his knee. The impact knocked him into a trench, where he lay unconscious for eight hours before medics found him and placed him on a litter. He remained there another six hours before finally being taken to a hospital.[208] Recovery was slow, and though he wanted to return to the front, he was invalided out of active duty and returned to New York in September.

Ted, commander of the Twenty-Sixth Infantry Regiment, First Battalion, First Division ("Pershing's Praetorian Guard") swallowed gas in the fight for Cantigny, a small action that assumed larger importance as it was the first offensive action taken by the American army. Despite the injury, he continued leading his men. When Eleanor finally saw him after the seesaw but finally successful fight for Cantigny, she wrote that he looked "ghastly."[209]

Nevertheless, he was back in action near Soissons during the Second Battle of the Marne as the AEF slowly, and with considerable cost, pushed the Germans from the salient they had carved out during their spring offensives. On July 19, 1918, Ted was hit by machine gun fire just above and behind his knee. Unable to locate a field ambulance—casualties were heavy everywhere—he managed to secure unofficial transportation and made his way back to Eleanor's Paris house in a dazed, near euphoric condition, likely caused by shock. Fortunately, brother-in-law Dick Derby, who had been recovering from "Flanders Flu," showed up and immediately recognized the wound as serious. "If it is not opened and cleaned out right away it will get infected and you might lose the leg," he told his reluctant brother-in-law.[210] Derby arranged transportation to the same hospital where Archie lay recovering from his injuries and assisted Colonel Joseph Blake, who operated on the leg. The limb was saved, and Ted would return to action, but he was left with no feeling in his heel and used a cane for the remainder of his life. Eleanor, Archie and Derby all regretted that the wound was not serious enough to earn a trip home.[211]

Kermit, who had won the Military Cross for his service with the British army in Iraq, transferred to the AEF in April 1918 and was posted to a field artillery unit in the First Division. His battery was among the many pounding the German lines as Ted and his fellow infantrymen launched

Ted and Eleanor Roosevelt, 1918. *Courtesy of the Library of Congress.*

their attacks. Having completed flight training at Hazelhurst, Quentin shipped out in July 1917 for France, where he spent a lengthy period in administrative work, though he sometimes managed to get to Paris to visit Eleanor and his siblings. In June, he was assigned to the First Air Pursuit Group, the "Kicking Mule" squadron, and began flying patrols over the front lines and dodging "archie"—antiaircraft fire.

Quentin Roosevelt, 1918. *Courtesy of the Library of Congress.*

On July 10, 1918, Quentin made a kill. Writing to Flora, he described coming upon German Pfalz monoplanes that "had white tails with black crosses....I was scared perfectly green, but then I thought to myself that I was so near I might as well take a crack at one of them."[212] Take a crack he did, and one of the Germans fell from the sky. Though the kill was unconfirmed, the plane having fallen behind German lines, Quentin was happy with his first performance under fire and celebrated with Eleanor in Paris. The next day, his squadron moved to a field near Rheims.

On July 14, Bastille Day, Quentin got into his second dogfight with German planes and was shot down and killed. The Germans buried him with military honors, though a German photographer took a picture of his body lying beside his broken aircraft. Since he had crashed behind German lines, his exact fate was initially uncertain. The first report to Sagamore Hill stated only that he was shot down and missing. Friends and family clung to the hope that he might have survived and been taken as a prisoner of war. TR was publicly stoic. In his official comment to the press on July 16, he stated tersely, "Quentin's mother and I are very glad that he got to the Front and had a chance to render some service to his country and show the stuff there was in him before his fate befell him."[213]

A day later, Harry Davison, accompanied by his son Trubee, still in the navy but incapable of flying duty, escorted a delegation from the Japanese Red Cross to visit the ex-president at Sagamore Hill. TR gave the visitors the expected tour of his home. But after the Japanese left, Trubee, who had been an acquaintance if not friend of the downed flyer, asked, "What hope have you for Quentin?" TR reached into his pocket and took out a piece of paper. "Trubee," TR said, "just twenty minutes before you arrived, I received this telegram from President Wilson." The message confirmed that Quentin was dead.[214]

Roosevelt was able to maintain outward composure in front of the public and non-family members, but inwardly, he was devastated. Already suffering from a variety of ailments, Quentin's death shook what physical and psychological reserves remained to TR. Though many believed him poised to achieve the greatest comeback in American political history, Roosevelt's health was deteriorating precipitously. Quentin's death delivered a body blow to his increasingly fragile body. He would be dead in six months.

In late July, Ted, Kermit and Archie gathered at Eleanor's house. Archie was still in a cast, while Ted was hobbling about on crutches. While they tried to show some cheer and conviviality, the shadow of the fallen Quentin rendered such gestures futile, and attempts to mask grief with alcohol only increased the strain. In the end, Ted and Kermit returned to their units, Ted as a newly promoted lieutenant colonel. Following the Armistice, he and Derby were sent with the American occupation forces guarding the bridges over the Rhine at Coblenz. As part of the Armistice terms, the Germans had agreed to allow British, French and American troops to control movement across the major crossings on the Rhine River, which effectively prevented Germany from renewing the war even defensively. Archie was invalided out and sailed for home in September, and it was he who telegraphed the poignant message to his brothers upon their father's death in January 1919: "The old lion is dead."[215]

Former secretary of war and activist Preparedness supporter Henry L. Stimson was second only to the Roosevelts in the ranks of prominent Long Islanders in military service. After training with the Seventy-Seventh Division, at Camp Upton, he arrived in France in advance of the division in January 1918 and was first attached to the British Fifty-First or Highland Division, where he attended a school for staff officers. A colonel in the Thirty-First Field Artillery, Stimson saw action in July 1918 as the Seventy-Seventh fought through the Aisne-Vesles lines. After five days on the front lines, he concluded that he had been under "more fire (little as it was) than many of the Civil War 'patriots' [GAR members] variety to whom we have so long looked up."[216]

Henry L. Stimson, circa 1918. *Courtesy of the Huntington Historical Society.*

Stimson was in combat throughout most of July and described himself as "wonderfully happy" because "the only thing worse than the fear that fills all the battlefields is the fear that fills the hearts of men who have not fought."[217] Though his time in action was relatively brief, his words indicate that he felt he had proven himself. He had been "blooded," had passed the test of manliness. Stimson would always think back on his military service with satisfaction and pride, and for the remainder of his life, he enjoyed being addressed as "colonel"—as had his friend, mentor and hero, Theodore Roosevelt.

James Ely Miller, circa 1917. *Courtesy of Bryon Derringer.*

Quentin Roosevelt was not the first Long Island aviator to fall in the Great War. That unhappy distinction went to James Ely Miller. Miller's background and career was similar to the Roosevelts in many ways. Not a member of what TR derided as the plutocracy, he sprang from a prominent Smithtown family with deep roots in the community. Born on March 24, 1883, he attended Berkley Prep School before proceeding on to Yale. There, as Trubee Davison and his fellow flyers did a decade later, he competed on the crew team and became a member of the prestigious Skull and Bones Society. After graduating summa cum laude in 1904, he entered the financial sector, rising to the position of vice president of the Columbia Trust Company and manager of its Manhattan branch.[218] He was also married with a daughter.

Typical for his class and background, Miller joined the Preparedness Movement and, like many young men, was drawn to aviation. He learned to fly in 1916, became a Reserve Military Aviator and subsequently helped to organize the First Reserve Aero Squadron. Upon the outbreak of hostilities, the Reserve Squadron was activated and trained as the United States Aero Squadron at Plattsburgh.[219]

Miller arrived in France in July 1917 and was appointed commanding officer of the Third Aviation Instruction Center at Issoudun, the base at which Quentin would later train. Like many flyers, Miller was anxious to see combat, and in March 1918, he flew to a French Spad squadron at Coincy, where he met two other Americans, Majors Johnson and Harmon, who were also hot to see action. The three men persuaded the French to let them fly Spads, the French Air Force's best combat fighter, in an unofficial "wildcat" patrol over the Champagne sector.

The mission soon went bad. Major Harmon's plane developed engine trouble, and he returned to Coincy. Miller, with Johnson as his wingman, was attacked by two German planes, including Germany's most advanced fighter, the Fokker DVII. The Americans evaded the attack but soon found two more German planes had joined the fight. Johnson broke off contact and flew home, leaving Miller on his own. He would later claim his guns had jammed.[220] Looking back, Johnson saw Miller's plane going into a spin above the forest of Corbeny.

Shot down by German Leutnant R. Hildebrand of Jagdstaffel (fighter squadron) 13, Miller was still alive when Hildebrand and another German officer reached the scene of the crash. The fallen American was taken to a German military hospital at Laon, where he soon died. According to Hildebrand and a German intelligence officer who were at his bedside,

Issoudun Air Field, France, circa 1918. *Courtesy of the Library of Congress.*

Miller lay at least part of the blame for his fate on Johnson.[221] On March 11, a German aircraft flew over the French base and dropped Miller's personal effects on the runway. After the fighting concluded in late 1918, Miller's body was removed from the German military cemetery where it was initially interred and reburied at the Oise-Aisne American military cemetery. Miller became the first American to die in aerial combat against an enemy while in United States service.[222]

Following the war, Miller Field on Staten Island was named in his honor. In 2017, Miller was posthumously awarded the Distinguished Flying Cross and Purple Heart, decorations that were not authorized until 1926 and 1932, respectively. His descendant Byron Derringer accepted the awards in his memory at a Pentagon ceremony in June of that year.

Tommy Hitchcock's dramatic exploits in the air ended on a happier note. The son of Thomas Hitchcock Sr., he grew up in the horse-centered world of Broad Hollow Farm in Old Westbury, but like many young Americans, he was also looking to the sky. Only seventeen when the United States finally declared war, he was denied admission to the Army Air Service on

Thomas Hitchcock
Jr., circa 1917.
*Courtesy of the Library
of Congress.*

account of his youth. He then managed to talk his way into the French Air Force, which waived its age requirement when he joined. With the American entry into the war, the Lafayette Escadrille was largely absorbed into the French Air Force, at which point many of its American members transferred to the United States service. Tommy remained among those who were still flying in French service.

By February 1918, the young American was flying combat missions over the front. His closest comrade was William Wellman, who would later win fame as a motion picture director. Wellman drew on his personal experiences for the classic World War I aviation epic *Wings.*

Tommy won his first victory on January 6, 1918, when he got the drop on a German plane and dove down on it, keeping up his fire until the enemy plane crashed.[223] A few days later, Hitchcock and Wellman double-teamed another German plane and chased it back to its airdrome. The German pilot managed to land safely and quickly scrambled out of his plane. But Wellman and Hitchcock were not through with him and pressed their attack. As reported in news accounts, "before the German had made three steps from his machine one of their bullets brought him down. The Americans returned to their own lines safely but with their machines full of shrapnel holes."[224]

Hitchcock and Wellman took down another German plane, an Albatross bomber, in mid-February. Writing to his parents, the twenty-one-year-old Wellman reported that he and Hitchcock were joined by a French flyer when they encountered the German bomber. But the Frenchman was unlucky. When he dove at the Albatross, his aircraft's wing snapped off, and he plummeted to earth. Unfazed, Tommy and Wellman continued the attack. Wellman wrote home that he and Hitchcock "tackled the Boche; first Tommy diving from above and coming up underneath him and shooting as near as possible, then I am repeating the performance."[225] The German plane began looping toward the ground with the two Americans attacking again and again. Wellman gave the Germans credit for "shooting back at us all the time," even while being forced down. The fight ended with the German plane crashing between the trench lines, after which the American pilots "started a lot of fun" strafing the German lines. "We were not touched, but the machines got it pretty badly."[226]

Their early successes made Hitchcock and Wellman minor celebrities at a time when American involvement seemed to progress slowly and ineffectively. The Lafayette Flying Corps Committee awarded them $100, while the French government decorated them with the Croix de Guerre with palms and, perhaps more importantly to young men, ten days' leave in Paris.[227]

Returning to his base, Hitchcock was soon in the air, where the Germans, who had apparently taken note of the aggressive American flyers, were intent on taking him down. Writing home, he described German attempts to lure him into an ambush. A plane he was pursuing began heading back to its own lines, with the German pilot feigning loss of power and control, dropping toward earth and inviting Hitchcock to follow. "I did not do any such thing," Tommy reported. "I kept on and then saw two German airplanes dart up from the ground, flying in my direction." The German decoy then began to climb and join the hunt for the American. "My gas was low," Tommy wrote to a relative, "and my ammunition was giving out so I made up my mind I would not give combat to the three Boches. I could not get one of these fellows but better work next time, maybe."[228]

Perhaps because they were incensed by Wellman and Hitchcock's machine gunning a pilot on the ground—unsportsmanlike behavior—the German pilots laid another ambush for the young Americans. On a patrol on March 6, Tommy spied two German planes below him and prepared to attack when another German aircraft, hiding above in the clouds, dove on him. The fight was over quickly. One bullet went through Hitchcock's side, while others cut his controls.

Hitchcock managed to land his shot-up plane in German territory, where he was immediately captured. The Germans treated him properly, as they did most Allied prisoners, and took him first to an aid station and then a military hospital near Saarbrucken. Prisoners of war were permitted limited mailing privileges through international organizations, and Tommy managed to send a postcard to a friend in Paris. In it, he gave a brief account of his last fight, capture and wound, which "is well now. You see it was not much."[229] He asked his friend to forward the message to his parents, which was quickly done. Though they knew he had been captured, it was the first word they had received directly from him.

Hitchcock later described the medical treatment at the hospital as only fair—1 doctor for every 150 patients. Additionally, the food was "not very good" and often in short supply, though he would later admit the German guards had little better.[230] As early as 1916, Germany faced chronic food shortages, a result of the British blockade, and Hitchcock, like other Allied prisoners, experienced it firsthand. The food he and the other POWs received through the international relief agencies was not only a welcome break from the monotonous and skimpy German rations, but it also proved a major element in keeping up health and body strength.

Tommy's wound was more serious than he let on in his postcard, and it took two months for it to heal sufficiently for him to be sent to regular POW camps in western Germany. Like many POWs, he kept looking for a chance to escape. His opportunity came when he was being transported by rail from a camp at Lechfeld to a new one at Rastatt. There was one German guard for three American prisoners, and when the train stopped at Ulm, the guard began to doze off. Tommy lifted a railway map and some money from the nodding guard, but the movement woke him up. The German quickly realized he had been pilfered, and Tommy, seeing it was now or never, grabbed his remaining rations and jumped from the train.

The German guard was unable to give chase lest the other two Americans bolt as well.[231]

Hitchcock then began a near one-hundred-mile odyssey—aided only by a small compass and what he knew of European geography—to take him to the Swiss border and safety. He slept during the daytime and covered as much ground as he could by night. He avoided towns and endeavored to sleep in woods when he could. He finally crossed into what he hoped was Switzerland and entered a small village where a girl who spoke French confirmed he had made it out of Germany. He did not remain long in Switzerland and returned to Paris, where he expressed his intention of transferring to American service. But the war ended before that could be arranged, and Tommy, like almost the entire AEF, shipped back to the United States, arriving in New York on November 14, 1918.

The Nassau County Board of Supervisors had hoped to stage "a suitable reception for a hero" to welcome Hitchcock back to Long Island. But the family opposed a public ceremony, and the young aviator's arrival in New York and return to Old Westbury was a strictly family affair.[232] In an interview he gave in December, Hitchcock stressed the importance of Red Cross food to himself and the other POWs. "I would never have escaped and walked 100 miles on the food supplied by the Germans. It was little packages of food supplied by the Red Cross which the Society succeeded in getting to me that gave me the strength to hike across the border and sufficient strength to plan my escape."[233] With the war over, Tommy, like all returning veterans, had to turn his attention to preparing himself for a peacetime life and career. As was true with many vets, it would not necessarily be an easy transition.

While American pilots dueled with their German opponents over the front, the Doughboys below slogged through mud, entrenchments, gas and machine gun fire to drive their still lethal foe from the territory they had earlier captured and push them back toward the German border.

In June 1918, as the German assaults again threatened Paris, American divisions began to enter the line, and the AEF came of age. Indeed, it proved decisive in halting the German offensives along the Marne that were aimed at the French capital. Once the last German offensives flickered out in July, the fresh and growing number of American troops undertook the counteroffensive in a campaign that in its entirety lasted somewhat over one hundred days before the Germans asked for an armistice.

With its own supplies and replacements dwindling, what reinforcements the German army received were often boys just finishing or not even finishing high school. Aware of the quarter million Americans arriving monthly and the massive amounts of material the Allies could muster, German morale began to plummet. Troops and civilians were also influenced by the spread of Bolshevik propaganda unleashed by the communist takeover of Russia in 1917, calling for an overthrow of the monarchy and an end to the war. The British naval blockade, now reinforced by the United States Navy, maintained its chokehold of German ports, resulting in widespread food shortages and malnutrition. In October 1918, the German homefront began to crack, and the German high command recognized it could not win the war or force a stalemated peace.

Ted and Archie Roosevelt were not the only prominent Long Islanders involved in the decisive battles of the summer and fall of 1918. Glen Cove resident F. Worthington Hine, president of the Keystone Powder Company and son of the president of the First National Bank, saw action as a lieutenant. He was slightly wounded in May 1918 as the AEF was just beginning to assume major combat operations.[234] The wound apparently did not keep him out of combat for long, for in July, he was caught in a gas attack and sent back to the United States to convalesce. His next, and last, assignment was Fort Sill in Oklahoma.[235]

Another resident of the Glen Cove–Lattingtown Military Industrial Complex to fight in his father's war was Lieutenant James J. Porter. His father, William H. Porter, was yet another Morgan partner, a friend and colleague of both Davison and Jack Morgan. Porter's estate overlooked Morgan's East Island mansion from the "mainland" of Glen Cove. Young Porter had attended Princeton and Harvard Law and was working as a lawyer on Wall Street when war was declared. Active in the Preparedness Movement, he was a member of Squadron A of the New York National Guard and had served on the border with Mexico after Pancho Villa's raids into New Mexico.

James Porter joined the regular army in 1917 and was initially assigned to a staff position. He requested a transfer to the front lines and was posted to the Tenth Machine Gun Battalion. James was serving with them when he was killed by artillery fire on October 5 during the Meuse-Argonne offensive. Edward R. Stettinius, who knew James's father at the Morgan Bank, was in France on War Department business when he saw the report of young Porter's death. Probably thinking a message from a friend was better than a government telegram, he took on the unpleasant duty of wiring the Porters that their twenty-seven-year-old son had been killed in action.[236]

Stettinius knew firsthand the anxiety parents and family suffered in worry over their children's fate in the war zones. His own son, William, had joined the colors in 1917. Though an aide to General Walter Gordon, he shared James Porter's desire to see action. He got it during the summer of 1918 as the AEF began its counterattack. He swallowed poison gas and was still recovering from the effects in September when his father visited him in a hospital near Chaumont. Unlike Porter, he would survive.[237]

Bradley Martin, an Old Westbury luminary married to Jay Phipps's sister, fought with the 77th Division, part of the recently organized National Army, as the draftee divisions were dubbed. Despite turning thirty-eight in 1918, Martin had volunteered for service and went through Officer Candidate School at Plattsburgh before being assigned to the 77th Division training at Camp Upton in the Suffolk County Pine Barrens. He sailed for France with the division on April 6, 1917, as a major in the 308th Regiment.

The 77th was the first of the National Army Division to be committed to action and was heavily engaged along the Aisne-Oise front, one of the series of fights that made up the Second Battle of the Marne. Bradley, though an adjutant in the 153rd Infantry Brigade—primarily a staff position—was often on the front lines and swallowed gas near Fismes on September 9. The injury was not considered serious, and he was back at the front when the 77th Division participated in the Meuse-Argonne offensive, the largest and most costly American campaign of the war.

The Meuse-Argonne campaign began on September 26 with an assault by most of the available U.S. combat divisions against the German lines along the Meuse. Some of the most desperate fighting took place in the dense Argonne Forest, where American troops assaulted well-prepared German defenses. The first phase of the battle ended on October 1 and then resumed on October 4, not really ending until the Armistice was signed on November 11. Though ultimately successful, driving the Germans from their well-concealed strong points in the heavily wooded and ravined forest resulted in heavy casualties. In the words of Geoffrey Wawro, General John J. "Pershing's insistence of 'push' [continuous frontal attack] had bled the army white," with virtually all the AEF's assault divisions requiring massive replacements.[238] During September and October 1918, the AEF suffered thirty-six thousand casualties per month, six times the monthly average in World War II.[239] "The three weeks after October 10 were the grittiest of the war," Wawro concluded, "the Germans throwing in the last of their first class divisions to hold their vital pivot [the German rail

Bradley Martin and family, circa 1918. *Courtesy of the Library of Congress.*

junction at Sedan] and the three American corps [of the AEF] measuring their daily advances in yards."[240]

The Meuse-Argonne also witnessed the ordeal of the Seventy-Seventh Division's "Lost Battalion." The battalion, led by New York lawyer Charles Whittelsey, was not actually lost but was cut off when surrounding units failed to keep up with it. For five days, the Lost Battalion was pounded by German artillery and ground down by continual sniping and direct attacks. Of the 670 men he had with him when first encircled, 191 remained alive and uninjured when Whittelsey was finally relieved.[241] Fortunately for Martin, he was not with Whittelsey's men but was engaged elsewhere in the Argonne, which was hot enough.

As costly as Pershing's tactics were, the increasing weight of the Allies, especially the growing size of the AEF and its aggressive tactics, forced the Germans from their best defensive positions. On October 24, American military intelligence reported that "for the first time in the history of the war the enemy has not one fresh division in reserve…which has been out of battle for more than a month."[242] Once the crucial German railroad juncture at Sedan was finally in Allied hands, the ability of the German army to move its troops effectively was erased. With revolution looming at home, Germany agreed to an armistice on Allied terms, with a subsequent peace conference to follow.

The Gold Coasters who served in the navy saw little direct action. The German surface fleet was bottled up in its bases by the British fleet. The U-boats, which had threatened the vital shipping lanes between America and Europe, were neutralized by the implementation of the convoy system. The United States Navy's most serious loss was the sinking of the cruiser USS *San Diego*, which struck a mine laid by a U-boat in the waters off Fire Island on the South Shore of Long Island. Fortunately, only six men were lost.

Junius Morgan, who had been handling the helm of a yacht since childhood, reported for active duty in the navy in April 1917. Fittingly, his first assignment was on his father's yacht, *Corsair*, engaged in coastal patrol. After a two-month stint at Navy Reserve Officers' Training Camp at Annapolis, he was assigned to the Queenstown patrol. The patrol was composed of U.S. destroyers that operated alongside British vessels stationed at Queenstown (now Cobh), Ireland. Serving on the USS *O'Brien*, Morgan participated in combination convoy escort/antisubmarine duty from the Irish Sea to Brest and the French Bay of Biscay ports.[243] In April, he was reassigned to the U.S. Naval Headquarters in London, where he was placed in charge of the Code and Signal section and acted as liaison with the British Admiralty for Communications.

Apparently, he was well suited for the task. In June, he was recalled to the States, where he took over the Code and Signal Department in Washington with a bump in rank to lieutenant jg (temporary). He received one last promotion in September, being advanced to full lieutenant, also temporary, as was the case with most Great War Reserve promotions. With the end of the war, the United States quickly began to reduce its military establishment, and with his service no longer in demand, Morgan resigned on December 13, 1918.

Perhaps the most experienced of the Gold Coast yachtsmen on active naval service was Robert E. Tod. Initially posted on the Morgan yacht *Corsair*, he made his most important contribution to the war ashore. In April 1918, Tod became commander of the Port Office at Brest on the west coast of France, one of the major landing bases for American troops and material. His responsibilities were expanded in August, when he was appointed the public works officer for the navy in all of France.[244] Tod upgraded the docking facilities, thereby increasing the overall effectiveness of the port.

Robert E. Tod on naval service, circa 1918. *Courtesy of the Library of Congress.*

Concerned that the water allowance provided by the French was inadequate, a shortcoming that slowed the deployment of transports, Tod personally donated $200,000 of his own money to build a water treatment plant capable of providing ten thousand gallons per day for personnel working or passing through Brest.[245]

Tod's contributions were recognized by both the French and American governments. France awarded him the Legion of Honor (officer grade), while Pershing presented him with a citation "for exceptionally meritorious and conspicuous services in Steamship Transportation A.E.F."[246] In 1920, the Navy Department bestowed the Navy Cross on Tod, citing his distinguished service "as Public Works Officer…in which capacity he performed especially meritorious service, especially in the establishment of a water supply at Brest."[247] Tod was also advanced in rank, receiving a promotion to commander shortly before his discharge in August 1919. By that time, virtually all the Gold Coast luminaries had returned to the United States, as the entire American Expeditionary Forces (minus Rhineland occupation units) was rapidly demobilized.

# CHAPTER 7

# SECOND ACTS

*W*ith the war over, victory won and peace apparently in hand, most of the Gold Coast's participants returned to their professional and personal pursuits. Some managed it relatively seamlessly, others less so. Indeed, for the most influential, the bankers and financiers, their wartime activities were largely an intensified and specialized extension of their peacetime professional activities. Consequently, their postwar careers constituted, in the words of Warren G. Harding, elected president in 1920, more "a return to normalcy" than anything else. This was most true for the Morgan bankers.

Jack Morgan, Harry Davison and Edward Stettinius were all in Europe in early 1919 engaged in related, if not identical, activities. Never forgetting to protect the family business, Jack Morgan made sure the bank had opportunities to invest in rebuilding the war-damaged European economies. Eventually, this came to include managing German war reparations (a key provision in the Treaty of Versailles). On a more personal note, he also donated his London residence to the United States government for use as an embassy.

For Harry Davison, the Great War was a transformative experience. Historian Priscilla Roberts described it best. "Davison," she wrote, "experienced something like a personal epiphany during the war, metamorphizing from a hard-driving businessman into an international philanthropist who developed ambitious schemes to remake the world."[248]

Harry Davison as head of the Red Cross War Committee with the Japanese delegation. Future Emperor Hirohito is on his left. *Courtesy of the Library of Congress.*

As head of the Red Cross War Council, Davison witnessed firsthand the devastation the war had inflicted on armies, civilians, economies and entire nations. His former tightly focused, near driven efforts to promote the interest of his firm and arrange, promote or coerce support for the Allies broadened to encompass the immediate and future needs of his nation and the world.

Davison's new agenda bemused some. One colleague described him as "just discovering labour, international relations and a lot of things…[and] having discovered them he thinks them all new."[249] Davison, of course, had learned a great deal about international relations during the war, though it was focused on support for Britain. The difference was that after 1918, he embraced the goals of international cooperation and humanitarian initiatives.

In 1919, Davison returned again to Europe, where he devoted most of his time engaging in negotiations with various Red Cross operations and visiting hospitals and battlefields. Davison's wartime experiences had led him to conclude that a permanent international organization was needed to deal with the global nature of the war's destruction and devastation. As a result of his efforts, the League of Red Cross Societies was founded with himself as president. Davison had hoped it would become "a real international Red Cross" and address global health issues such as tuberculosis, plague, yellow fever and typhus.[250] Wilson and his personal advisor Colonel Edward House supported the idea and brought it up in discussions with British prime minister David Lloyd-George. The new effort foundered when the U.S. and European Red Cross organizations withheld their support, and the league was ultimately absorbed by the International Committee of the Red Cross.[251] Though disappointed in the outcome, Davison remained convinced that his objectives would ultimately triumph. Time would prove him right.

Like Jack Morgan and Lamont, Davison was deeply concerned with European economic reconstruction, which he believed more important than the political settlement. His career in banking and finance had taught him that no enduring peace could be achieved among nations whose economies were weak and unstable. His solution was a program of short- and long-term aid for Europe, which anticipated the later Marshall Plan. Perhaps more surprisingly, he opposed a punitive peace on Germany and supported Wilson's League of Nations. Though a lifelong Republican, he denounced his party's opposition to the League as "perfectly incomprehensible."[252] During the 1920 presidential election, he reluctantly supported the Republican candidate, Warren G. Harding, whose promise of a "return to normalcy" prescribed less, rather than more, international involvement by the United States.

In no way did Davison's newfound embrace of international cooperation diminish his faith in Anglo-Saxon superiority. Indeed, his wartime experiences, including time spent among convivial British imperial apparatchiks, strengthened and deepened his commitment to Anglo-American leadership in a more globalist age.[253] Anglo-American partnership had been essential to winning the war, and that partnership, cultivated and nurtured by men such as himself, was equally necessary for an enduring peace.

Stettinius was in Europe by the summer of 1918 as one of the American representatives to the Inter-Allied Munitions Council. He remained in Europe after the Armistice, helping liquidate contracts with the British and French.[254] Company business was not neglected, and Stettinius initiated measures intended to revitalize the Morgan Company's Paris office. The munitions master also devoted time to scout out investment opportunities, working in concert with Davison, who was back in New York ready to arrange necessary financing.[255] Before he returned to the United States, Stettinius received the Distinguished Service Medal from Secretary of War Newton Baker in recognition of his role in the "procurement of munitions both [in the United States] and abroad."[256] The following June, France made him a commander in the Legion of Honor.

The conclusion of the Great War did not end the violence. Nor did all those who nursed grievances against the Morgan Bank suddenly change their minds. On September 16, 1920, New York experienced the deadliest terrorist attack on American soil before 9/11. A bomb that had been placed in a horse-drawn cart exploded directly in front of the Morgan offices on Wall Street. Thirty-eight people were killed and many more wounded. Jack Morgan was away on a trip to England, and neither Stettinius nor Davison was present. But Junius, who had entered the family business after leaving the navy, was wounded by flying glass, though not enough to keep him from a luncheon appointment.[257] Though Junius escaped with only minor injuries, William Joyce, a clerk who had been sitting near the front window, was killed.

The attack on Wall Street, particularly its symbolic center—the Morgan Bank—fed into the "Red Scare," a nationwide wave of anxiety that was fanned by some federal officials, especially Attorney General A. Mitchell Palmer. The bombing and instances of alleged radical labor disruption

Explosion at the Morgan Bank, 1920. *Courtesy of the Library of Congress.*

were blamed on Bolshevik (Communist) agents or agitators directed by the Communist regime that had recently seized power in Russia. Though no one was ever charged in connection with the Wall Street bombing, the perpetrators were most likely anarchists, members of a political movement that had carried out a number of bombings and assassinations between 1880 and 1920. Following the mass arrests of people who were subsequently released due to lack of any evidence, and the failure of a predicted uprising by Bolsheviks, the Red Scare faded away. But Palmer's subordinate, J. Edgar Hoover, who ran the Justice Department's G Division, was just beginning his career.

Upon his return to New York in 1920, Stettinius began a search for a new and permanent family home, focusing on Long Island. He had gained firsthand knowledge of Long Island during the war when he relocated his family there due to fears of an assassination or kidnapping attempt by German agents. In 1921, he decided to put down roots in the North Shore Gold Coast and purchased the estate of the Viscountess H.Y. deLendonck, the widow of Levi C. Weir. Stettinius was already familiar with his new abode, having rented it in 1916.

Located in Lattingtown, his new residence placed him in neighborly proximity with Davison, Jack Morgan and an extensive network of Old Stock/Gold Coast luminaries. With his connections and well-regarded wartime career, the munitions czar easily entered into the social life of the area and became a member of the tony Creek and Piping Rock Clubs. While not the most opulent property on the Gold Coast, the Shelters, as he christened his new residence, met the area standards for comfort and respectability. Figures from 1924 reveal an outlay of $250,000 to run the estate, which employed nine full-time gardeners and had six cars on hand for family use.[258]

In 1922, Stettinius made his most enduring contribution to the Gold Coast society. He noticed a sizable stretch of vacant land adjoining what was then a small burial ground alongside the Locust Valley Reformed Church. Stettinius bought the land, effectively took over the board of directors of the original church grounds and created the Locust Valley Cemetery. He then set about creating a suitable resting place for families of wealth and distinction along the lines of the carefully planned "garden" or "rural" cemeteries that had become popular during the nineteenth century. The Olmsted Brothers firm laid out the new sections and selected the plantings, while the architectural flourishes were designed by the high-profile firm of Walker and Gillette. In the words of Stettinius biographer John Douglas

Forbes, "The new section of woods and spacious glades became a Valhalla for Morgan partners and their friends."[259] Indeed, the cemetery's expanded board was dominated by Morgan-connected businessmen, including Paul Pennoyer, Jack Morgan's son-in-law; Trubee Davison; Artemus L. Gates, a Yale Aero Squadron veteran and Harry Davison's son-in-law; Robert A. Lovett, also a Yale Aero Squadron alumnus and son of financier Robert Lovett; plus Lyman N. Hine and Stettinius himself.

But Stettinius was not the first of the major Gold Coast wartime players to require the new cemetery's offerings. By 1921, Harry Davison began to show signs of ill health, including exhaustion and headaches. Physicians soon diagnosed a brain tumor. He underwent an operation in August 1921 that brought him some relief, though the tumor could not be fully removed. He was visibly declining by the following spring. On May 5, 1922, his doctors decided that an immediate operation was necessary, and an operating room was arranged on the second floor of the Peacock Point estate.[260] Family members and business partners, including Jack Morgan, gathered in the house or on the grounds waiting for word from the surgeons. The news was grim. The operation failed, and Davison died on May 6, 1922. His estate, when probated in 1925, totaled $8,111,548.[261] His widow was given

Davison family plot, Locust Valley Cemetery. *Author's collection.*

a life share of over $6 million, with Trubee to inherit $4.5 million upon his mother's decease.[262]

More than five hundred people gathered at St. John's of Lattingtown for Davison's funeral services. Both the church pews and outside seating were filled, and many sat on the surrounding lawns as local police and private security directed traffic and parking.[263] Family members honored Harry's wishes and did not wear black to the service. All Morgan partners, except Lamont and Junius Morgan, who were overseas, were in attendance.[264] Following the services, Davison was laid to rest in the family plot in the Locust Valley Cemetery.

Harry Davison's belief in the viability and desirability of an Anglo-Saxon partnership between the United States and Britain had never wavered. Indeed, fed by his close, cordial relations with British politicians, bankers and businessmen, it deepened during the war. He considered such an alliance essential for Allied triumph and equally important for a stable, prosperous peace in the postwar world.[265] Though the term postdates him, he was an early and passionate supporter of the "special relationship" between the two nations. Indeed, his suggestion that Britain apply pressure on the Wilson administration by ceasing purchases of war materials after the Federal Reserve Board blocked his proposed sale of British Treasury notes in 1916 raises the question of how far his interests and loyalties had become inseparable from those of his ancestral and idealized country.

In the few years he had left after the Armistice and peace treaty, Davison began devising a method to further Anglo-American comity along the lines first laid out by Cecil Rhodes. His intent was to create a scholarship to enable British students to "know what America really is."[266] In a personal—familial—way, he had earlier attempted to strengthen the bond of WASP solidarity by sending one of his sons to Cambridge for a year, "not to take an English degree, but in order to get an insight into English life."[267]

Davison died before he could fully formulate his plans, but his wife, Kate, took up the cause in his memory. In April 1925, she unveiled the Henry P. Davison Scholarship Fund, which set up a trust to allow six British university students—three each from Oxford and Cambridge—to attend either Harvard, Yale or Princeton for at least one year.[268]

Though he became master of Peacock Point upon his father's death, Trubee Davison's appetite for public service remained keen.[269] Although the accident that ended his flying career made walking difficult, he embarked on a multifaceted career in government that spanned three decades. During the Republican ascendancy of the 1920s, Trubee served several terms as New

York State assemblyman before Calvin Coolidge appointed him chairman of the National Crime Commission. He was then named assistant secretary of war for air, likely a more congenial slot, as his passion for aviation remained undimmed. He held the job until Franklin Roosevelt took office in 1933. When the Central Intelligence Agency was established after World War II, Trubee served as its first director of personnel. He was also heavily involved with the American Museum of Natural History, becoming a trustee in 1922 and president in 1933. He retired from his museum responsibilities when he accepted the CIA position in 1951.[270]

Trubee never forgot the excitement and camaraderie of the Millionaires' Unit, and the estate became the site of annual summer reunions for Yale Aero Unit members. Among these was Artemis "Di" Gates, who had married Trubee's sister. His brother Harry Jr., who had won a Navy Cross in air combat over Belgium, was a director of *Time* magazine before joining his father's old firm, J.P. Morgan and Sons. A partner in 1929, he was later senior vice president, president and vice chairman of the reorganized Morgan Guaranty Trust.[271] In 1942, Harry was recalled to the navy and placed in charge of the Air Combat Intelligence School in Quonset, Rhode Island, before appointment to the command of operational intelligence in the Pacific Fleet.[272] Harry died in 1961 and Trubee thirteen years later. Along with their wives and Gates, they were buried in the family plot in Locust Valley Cemetery.

Edward Stettinius himself did not have long to enjoy his home and handiwork. He underwent an operation for appendicitis in August 1920 and never fully recovered. He fell seriously ill in 1922 with what became increasingly painful abdominal ailments. At times, he sought relief vacationing along the Penobscot Bay or the spas at White Sulphur Springs, West Virginia. He traveled to and from New York and White Sulphur Springs on a private railroad car named *Peacock Point* that was originally owned by Harry Davison and later by the Morgan Bank, which placed it at Stettinius's disposal.[273]

As his decline continued, Stettinius kept close to his home in Lattingtown. In March 1925, he underwent an operation for intestinal abscesses. Despite his weakened condition, he managed to take a short cruise on Morgan's *Corsair* in July 1925. But the decline was irreversible, and he died of a cerebral embolism on September 3, 1925, at the Shelters. Jack and Junius Morgan, Thomas Lamont and other friends and colleagues attended the funeral services, which were held at the house. He left a taxable estate of $5 million. His wife and children had previously been given trusts totaling a further $2.5 million.[274] Stettinius was buried in plot seven of the cemetery he

Edward R. Stettinius grave slab, Locust Valley Cemetery. *Author's collection.*

had—perhaps with a sense of his impending mortality—created. It is a short walking distance from Davison's grave site.[275]

Many considered Stettinius a delayed casualty of the war, his death caused by the long hours of work while pushing himself unsparingly to produce and secure materials of war for the western Allies. The *New York Times* opined that he "labored so prodigiously for the Allies and later for this country that he undermined his own health and when he underwent an operation for appendicitis in August 1920, he never fully recovered."[276] Thomas Lamont, who had worked closely with him at the Morgan Bank, concurred. "[I]f ever a man laid down his life for a cause," he later wrote, "it was Edward Stettinius. Never sparing himself mentally or physically, he worked under superhuman burdens during the five years from 1915 to 1920. His health could not endure the strain."[277]

Jack Morgan continued as head of the Morgan Bank after the war and oversaw the conversion of his father's library, including its outstanding rare book and manuscript collection, into a publicly accessible institution. He weathered the hostile criticism directed at the bank in the 1930s and died on March 13, 1943. His estate was officially estimated at $60 million at the time of his death.[278] A company appraisal in 1947 revised the figure sharply downward to $4,642,791.[279] Matinecock Point, the Morgan estate in Glen Cove, was sold after his death and later became a retreat house for a Catholic religious order. When it was demolished in 1980, only 3 of the original 257 acres remained.[280] The rest had been converted into suburban houses, a fate that awaited the remnant property.

Professionally, Junius Morgan devoted himself to the family banking business between the wars. Maritime pursuits dominated his leisure activities. He was commodore of the New York Yacht Club from 1933 to 1935 (a position his father and grandfather had also held) and was directly involved in the America's Cup races.[281] As a trustee of the American Museum of Natural History, he focused on matters oceanic. Morgan never severed his connection with the navy and held a position in the navy reserve as well as membership in the New York Commandery of the Naval Order of the United States.

Morgan was recalled to active duty shortly before Pearl Harbor and was promoted to commodore in August 1942. Perhaps his experience with codes during the Great War led to his assignment with the Office of Strategic Services, the immediate forerunner of the Central Intelligence Agency. He returned to private life at the war's conclusion, having risen to the rank of captain. Morgan died from an attack of ulcers on October 19, 1960, while on a hunting trip in Ontario. A funeral service was held at St. John's of Lattingtown three days later with interment in the family plot in Hartford, Connecticut. The estate he built on the opposite end of East Island from his father's, Salutations, remains intact, though it is no longer in family hands.

Robert Tod, another ardent yachtsman, served as commissioner of immigration in New York during the Harding administration (1921–23.) Following that last stint of public service, he spent most of his time at his Syosset estate. His daughter married H. Bradley Martin, son of Bradley Martin, owner of Knole, forming yet another union of Gold Coast families.

In 1944, Tod was stricken by brucellosis, a disease contracted through contact with infected animals or their products. The disease is characterized by undulant fever, which spikes and falls, as headaches, chills, sweats and backpain add further torments to the victims. While Todd was struggling with the infection, he received word that the government had rejected his offer of wartime service. Likely descending into the black hole of depression,

Matinecock Point, the J.P. Morgan estate, was demolished in 1980. *Courtesy of the Glen Cove Public Library Robert R. Coles Long Island History Room.*

he shot himself at his Long Island home. A surprisingly detailed *New York Times* obituary reported that his daughter heard the shot and "rushed to find her father's body lying on the floor, a bullet through the head and the weapon beside him."[282] He was buried in the family plot at Green-Wood Cemetery in Brooklyn.

Ted Roosevelt Jr remained in Europe for a time following the Armistice. The terms of the ceasefire called for the establishment of three zones of occupation—British, French and American—to control the major Rhine River crossings. This was intended to prevent Germany from launching a counteroffensive (impossible under the circumstances) and allowing the Allies to push deeper into Germany should its new government refuse to accept the terms of the ensuing peace treaty. Ted's division, the First, was part of the initial occupation force.

Ted's Jr time in occupied Germany did not last long. But before he returned to the United States, he, Stimson and William "Wild Bill" Donovan, Medal of Honor winner and future OSS chief, began discussing a meaningful postwar role for AEF veterans. These conversations became the foundation of what remains the United States' largest veterans' organization, the American Legion. The process was approved by a convention of about one thousand veterans who supported the plan to channel the patriotism and dedication of the troops into peacetime purposes. It seems likely that they took the Grand Army of the Republic (GAR), established by Union Civil War veterans after 1865, as their model. They believed the AEF's spirit could be harnessed to advance useful government policy, further the needs of veterans and provide an ongoing vehicle for comradeship and social life. While the guns on the Western Front were still cooling, the American Legion was already emerging as a force of national importance.

Back in America, Ted Jr. attempted to follow his father's footsteps by entering politics. He won a seat in the New York Assembly but quickly accepted the post of assistant secretary of the navy in 1921—his father's first major governmental position. He was poised for a run at the New York governor's chair in 1924 when he was blindsided by the Teapot Dome scandal. The scandal involved the sale of a government petroleum reserve, the Teapot Dome, formerly controlled by the navy, to private interests. Transferred to the Department of Interior's administration, the reserve was surreptitiously sold to the Sinclair Oil Corporation, where Archie had secured a position.

Neither Roosevelt had any involvement in the corrupt bargain, and Ted was subsequently exonerated by a Senate inquiry. Nevertheless, their names were among the most notable to appear in government investigations and the press. The scandal hung like a cloud over Ted's gubernatorial candidacy. The race became personally bitter when Eleanor, wife of Democrat Franklin D. Roosevelt, enthusiastically enlisted in the campaign to defeat her Republican cousin, initiating a split between the Sagamore Hill and Hyde Park branches of the Roosevelts that was a long time in healing.[283]

Defeated in his first major political outing, and lacking his father's gifts, Ted's subsequent public service came through appointed office. He served ably as governor general of first Puerto Rico and later the Philippines during the Hoover administration. When his distant cousin Franklin D. Roosevelt became president in 1933, Ted knew his tenure was up. Asked about his relationship with the new president during an interview, he replied, "Fifth cousin, about to be removed."[284] Ted saved FDR the trouble and resigned.

Ted Jr. had remained in the army reserve throughout the 1920s and '30s, and once the United States entered the Second World War, he resumed active duty. He fought in the Mediterranean theater from North Africa through Sicily. Although he was already suffering from a serious heart

Brigadier General Theodore Roosevelt Jr., circa 1943. *Courtesy of Sagamore Hill National Historic Site, National Park Service, Oyster Bay, New York.*

condition, he was the only general officer to land with the troops on Utah Beach at Normandy on D-Day, June 6, 1944. Under heavy German fire, he directed incoming troops to their positions and kept up their nerves and spirits with references to his father. He was slated for a divisional command when he died of a heart attack on July 15, 1944. Ted was buried at the American Cemetery in Normandy. After the war, his brother Quentin was disinterred from his resting place and buried next to him. For his actions on the Normandy beaches, Ted was posthumously awarded the Medal of Honor.

Archie also returned to active service. After a great deal of cajoling, the army agreed to send him to the hot, humid rainforests of New Guinea, where he fought in MacArthur's campaign to drive the Japanese from its coast. Like his brother, Archie bucked up the young soldiers' morale with stories of his father and his own serious wounding in the Great War. "You're safe with me," he assured his men, twenty-plus years younger than him. "I was wounded three times in the last war and that's a lucky charm."[285] But the heat, humidity, malaria and effects of his earlier wounds wore down his middle-aged body, and he was finally withdrawn from combat and given a

*Left*: Archie Roosevelt (*left*) in the Pacific, circa 1944. *Courtesy of the Library of Congress.*

*Right*: Kermit Roosevelt, World War II, circa 1942. *Courtesy of Sagamore Hill National Historic Site, National Park Service, Oyster Bay, New York.*

medical discharge. He was the only American soldier to be released with a 100 percent disability in both world wars.

Following the war, Archie resided in Cold Spring Harbor, twenty minutes away from his boyhood home at Sagamore Hill. After his wife was killed in an automobile accident, he moved permanently to his winter home in Florida, where he died in 1962.

Time had not been kind to Kermit Roosevelt. By the end of the 1930s, his drinking had degenerated into alcoholism, and his marriage shattered as he took up with another woman. Nevertheless, he became the first of the Roosevelt brothers to see combat in the Second World War. While the United States was still officially neutral in 1939–41, Kermit repeated his Great War precedent, joined the British army and took part in Britain's failed Narvik Expedition in Norway. He then returned to the United States, drinking heavily and often out of contact with members of his family. Kermit's long-suffering wife appealed to FDR for help in locating him, and FBI agents tracked his whereabouts. The president's aid proved a first step in the lengthy process of rapprochement between the two Roosevelt clans.

Ethel Roosevelt in Red Cross uniform, circa 1945. *Courtesy of Sagamore Hill National Historic Site, National Park Service, Oyster Bay, New York.*

Meanwhile, remaining plagued by acute alcoholism probably exacerbated by underlying depression, Kermit had returned to the American army. In an attempt to keep him from the temptations of large city life with its nightclubs and bars, Kermit was posted to Fort Richardson in Alaska. He shot himself to death on June 3, 1943. His mother, Edith, was told he died of a heart attack.

Ethel Derby and Eleanor Butler Alexander Roosevelt did their Second World War service by supporting the Red Cross at home. Eleanor died in 1962 and Ethel in 1977, thirteen years after her husband, Dick Derby.

Upon his return from the war, Bradley Martin settled into the comforts of Knole, his Old Westbury estate, and resumed his career in finance. He was an officeholder in the Hudson Trust and also served on the board of the Bessemer Trust and Company, a Phipps family affiliate, to which he was connected through his wife, Helen Phipps. Though he did not seek publicity, Martin was an active philanthropist, serving as president and director of the Tuberculosis Preventorium for Children (later Child Care Center). He was also vice president of the Nassau County Hospital Association. Typical for his class and time, he was an active clubman. Martin kept abreast of his wartime comrades through his membership in the Seventy-Seventh Division Association.[286] He died at Knole on June 3, 1963.

After he returned to Broad Hollow Farm in Old Westbury, Tommy Hitchcock, not quite nineteen, seemed unsure of his next steps in life—not surprising, considering his wartime experiences. Without much enthusiasm, he returned to Harvard, where he received his degree despite a lackluster academic performance. On December 15, 1928, he married Margaret "Peggy" Mellon Loughlin, a widow with a son. A year later, he bought his own estate at Sands Point, one of the northern necks characterizing large parts of the Gold Coast.

Tommy gravitated into finance after college, eventually joining Lehman Brothers in 1932. But his real profession, and passion, was polo. Indeed,

Tommy Hitchcock (*center*) in action. Piping Rock Club, July 23, 1930. *Author's collection.*

his dominance on the playing fields turned what was considered a rich man's game into a popular spectator sport. As the *New York Times* wrote after his death, "He fired the American imagination more than any polo player ever had" and is "generally considered the greatest in the history of the sport."[287] A ten-goal player for most of his career, he led American teams to repeated triumphs in international competition before retiring from professional polo in 1940.

Despite his love and passion for the game, there was one contest that he held in greater esteem. "Polo," he said in a 1938 interview, "is exciting, but you can't compare it to flying in wartime. That was the best sport in the world....People call duck hunting sport because they get the thrill of shooting something down. It's not real sport unless the duck can shoot back at you.—That's what flying was during the war. It was exciting because I was young, but I wouldn't enjoy the flying and fighting now—it would be a painful duty."[288]

But it was one he would accept after the United States entered the Second World War in December 1941. Hitchcock then joined the Army Air Corps and was posted to Britain. He became involved with the development of the P-51 Mustang and, despite his relatively advanced age of forty-four, was cleared for combat flying in the spring of 1944, at which time he was appointed commander of a Mustang fighter group in the Ninth Air Force.

Hitchcock was concerned by the number of unexplained crashes of the new fighter and suspected that the engines were not powerful enough for the

Mustang's requirements. Out on a test flight on April 19, 1944, Hitchcock put his P-51 into a dive but was unable to pull out and crashed. Subsequent to his death, the Mustang was outfitted with Rolls-Royce engines that gave the aircraft the power it needed to fulfil its potential and become the best all-around fighter plane of the war.[289]

Tommy Hitchcock left an estate of $1,847,120.31 net, to his widow, Margaret Mellon Hitchcock. A sizable chunk of that would be eaten up by the New York State inheritance tax, estimated at $97,975.99.[290] Margaret received all real estate and tangible personal property, with the residual placed in trust for their children.[291]

Between the wars, as the euphoria of 1918–19 faded, a certain sense of unease and disillusionment entered American thinking about its participation in the Great War. Some of this was traceable to the highly idealistic war aims that the government embraced upon America's entry into the conflict. The 1920s had barely begun when it was apparent that the war hadn't ended all wars and the world was not safe for democracy. Others began to look at American trade, especially the sale of arms and

Army Air Corps lieutenant colonel Tommy Hitchcock in New York before returning to Britain, December 1943. *Author's collection.*

munitions, as a major factor in bringing the nation into the conflagration. From there, it was a short step in questioning the role of large banks and industries in pushing the trade and their influence in government decisions about the war. Such misgivings and a sense of having been stampeded into the conflict for the benefit of corporate and financial millionaires grew when the Great Depression hit in 1929. A sour, skeptical—if not cynical— attitude began to spread, even among veterans. As proud as they were of their service, many began to question how they ended up in France. Or whether their sacrifices were worth it.

Davison and Stettinius were dead when the Nye Committee opened hearings on the role of financial and industrial giants in the American entry into the war. Junius Morgan played no major role at the hearings, though his father, Jack, provided testimony. It was left to Tommy Lamont, the bank's effective CEO following Davison's death, to take on the role of major defender of the Morgan Bank's activities during the period of American neutrality. Combative and condescending, Lamont parried the thrusts of the questioners, who were hampered by the overwhelming complexity of the evidence. That the Morgan Bank operated a foreign trade and munitions operation as large, or larger, than many countries was obvious. But to what degree did the financiers influence government decision making? Or were they simply implementing the program the Wilson administration desired but would not admit publicly? Interestingly, when the committee members began to turn their attention to Woodrow Wilson's own actions, the investigation was shut down.[292] After all, the Democrats controlled both houses of Congress and the presidency, and there was no appetite to reveal any failures on the part of a recent president who was still considered a party hero. Despite the inconclusive nature of the proceedings, the Nye Committee amassed a mountain of information detailing the outsized role of Morgan, its partners and fellow travelers—well ensconced along the Gold Coast—in influencing policy and opinion in favor of the Allies and providing them with the materials they needed to survive and pursue the war.

Indeed, some of those who had been most enthusiastic about the American entry into World War I, and who had fought in it, were hesitant for the country to repeat the performance as war loomed in 1939–41. Tommy Hitchcock initially thought the United States should stay out. Ted Roosevelt felt likewise and was for a time a member of the America First Committee. America First took the position—going back to George Washington—that Europe was almost always at war and the United States derived little advantage from getting involved. Certainly, Hitchcock and Roosevelt had seen war close up and were not eager to see their countrymen—and children—go through the same experiences. After the United States went to war, America First was seen by many as a tainted organization, its noninterventionist stance denounced as myopic and favorable to the Axis enemy. There was also an anti-Semitic streak in the movement that further alienated many Americans, especially as the realities of the Holocaust were revealed.

But in the 1939–41 period, most noninterventionists believed that the nation had been bamboozled and had joined the Great War out of a combination of naïve idealism, skillful propaganda and the machinations of the financial-industrial complex. Such views began to shift as the fate of the democracies grew dire and the power and nature of the Axis clearer. Ted Roosevelt quit America First when its leadership criticized arming for defense, and Tommy joined the U.S. Army Air Corps once the country was fully committed. In that way, they were like most intervention skeptics. Pearl Harbor changed everything.

Of all the Gold Coast's major figures, none had a more distinguished post-1918 career than Henry Stimson. As a celebrity veteran just after the Armistice in 1918, he was invited by New York mayor "Red Mike" Hylan to join a municipal committee in charge of arranging suitable welcome home ceremonies for the troops. Instead, Stimson joined several other Republicans in declining the offer, citing the presence of publishing magnate William Randolph Hearst on the committee for their refusal. In contrast to his interventionist—if not jingoist—attitude in 1898, Hearst, through his newspaper empire, had sought to keep the United States out of the war. Speaking for many, Stimson wrote Hylan that he would not care "to be welcomed by such a man who has assumed such an attitude towards the war, and towards the gallant Allies whom I saw fighting for our cause. I think the great majority of my comrades in the A.E.F. would feel the same way." Though Stimson turned down the proffered committee position, he stated he was willing "to perform my share in the welcome of our returning soldiers through the medium of unofficial but more appropriately constituted committees of welcome."[293]

Indeed, he was most agreeable to take part in welcome home ceremonies in his hometown of Huntington. The town organized four separate welcome home events as troops were discharged from service. The second such event on February 28, 1919, featured dinners, a vaudeville show, the bestowal of town victory medals and an ovation by Stimson.[294]

Stimson resumed his lucrative law practice and life at his Manhattan apartment and estate at Highhold in West Hills. Indeed, he lost no time in resuming the Thanksgiving "Highhold Games" and continued his traditional practice of extending an open invitation to all friends and neighbors. He received some negative press for hosting the first postwar games at exactly the same time Thanksgiving services were held in Huntington's churches. "SWC," writing in the "Out on Long Island" section for the *Brooklyn Eagle*, wrote, "We very much fear that the attendance at the Stimson farm approximated that at the services in the Huntington churches."[295] Clearly, "SWC" feared they exceeded the attendance at divine worship. Neither Stimson nor the game-goers appears to have cared.[296]

Stimson returned to public life as governor general of the Philippines and secretary of state in the Hoover administration. As he had done during the Great War, he was an outspoken proponent of rearmament and support for the Allies in the perilous years between 1939 and 1941. His support for Franklin Roosevelt's measures to bolster Britain and place the United States on a war footing did not go unnoticed. Roosevelt had learned from Woodrow Wilson's exclusion of Republicans from key decisions in 1917–19 and sought bipartisan support for his military and foreign policy measures. Though a lifelong Republican, Stimson was on the same page as Roosevelt regarding the war, and with a proven record in war and diplomacy, he was a perfect choice for secretary of war in a national unity government.

When FDR offered him the post on July 20, 1940, Stimson immediately accepted. He brought his energy, commitment and intelligence to a position that involved him in every major decision made by the United States during World War II, including the development and ultimately the use of the atomic bomb. Among his fellow cabinet members were Edward R. Stettinius Jr., eldest son of Davison's munitions chief, who served as secretary of state in 1944–45 and United States representative to the United Nations in 1945–46. Robert Lovett, a veteran of the Yale Aero Squadron and Lattingtown resident, was assistant secretary of war for the Army Air Corps. The War Department under Stimson took on a very Gold Coast character.

Stimson remained in his post as secretary of war after Harry Truman succeeded to the presidency. With the war successfully concluded, and conscious of his failing health, Stimson resigned in September 1945. Though he authorized the use of atomic weapons to force Japanese surrender, he advocated placing the new, destructive technology under international control in the postwar era. In recognition of his indefatigable service during the war, Truman awarded Stimson the Distinguished Service Medal. At the presentation ceremonies, Truman read a citation noting Stimson's long and stellar career:

Secretary of War Henry L. Stimson (*left*) and Secretary of War for Air, former Yale Aero Squad member and Lattingtown resident Robert Lovett. *Courtesy of the Huntington Historical Society.*

*Following 40 years of conspicuous public service in which he fought as a combat officer in one war and twice served in the cabinets of presidents, Mr. Stimson unhesitatingly accepted the vast responsibility for the development of the American armies to play a determining part in the desperate human conflict now victoriously terminated.*

*His fearlessness, his integrity, his rich experience, his wisdom and his statesmanship were largely contributory to the successful mobilization, deployment and operations of an Army in which his countrymen may take everlasting pride. His steadfast purpose and unselfish devotion were an inspiration to men-at-arms in American forces throughout the world in their bitter fight to maintain moral right, freedom, justice and civilization itself.*[297]

Having completed his last, and most significant, public service, Stimson returned to Highhold which, as he wrote a year before his death, "was the real home."[298] On September 21, 1947, a near pantheon of American

Highhold, Henry Stimson's estate in the West Hills, Huntington. *Courtesy of the Huntington Historical Society.*

military and diplomatic notables arrived at Highhold to congratulate him on his eightieth birthday. Among the distinguished well-wishers were national icons including Army Chief of Staff and Secretary of State General George C. Marshall, General Dwight D. Eisenhower, Army Air Forces Commander Carl Spaatz, General Courtney Hodges and foreign policy advisors Harvey and McGeorge Bundy. Marshall read a personal message from Truman that again noted his many contributions to the war before concluding, "I affectionately and respectfully salute you Mr. Secretary, our distinguished friend and leader, on your eightieth birthday."[299] Stimson died in 1950 and was buried in the Memorial Cemetery of St. John's Church of Cold Spring Harbor.[300]

Though some of the North Shore luminaries continued on, Stimson's death marked the end of an epoch. In many ways, the halcyon days of the generation that led the nation into the Great War, fought it and returned for an encore during the Second World War died with him. It also marked an end to the dominance of the WASP ethos that the Gold Coast mandarins encapsulated and personified. Their conception of the nation and national greatness simultaneously idealized and limited—their *Weltanschauung*—reverberated for another twenty years before being challenged, often derided, by competing, often hostile counter-assumptions. The latter shattered the WASP interpretation of American history and the American future without replacing it with a national narrative of equal value and utility.

# CHAPTER 8

# THE VIEW FROM OLYMPUS

*T*he near uniformity of outlook regarding the Great War's belligerent powers that characterized the thinking and actions of the Gold Coast—and generally northeastern—elites sprang from several mutually reinforcing elements. Certainly, economic and financial interest, both immediately and in the perceived future, played a role. Gold Coast personalities from the Morgan network to people like the Phippses, Hitchcocks, Tods, Stimsons and Roosevelts all believed the Allies would prevail, and siding with them put American companies, and the United States generally, in an advantageous position to profit—economically and geopolitically—from such a triumph. Indeed, the financial, business and personal associations formed during the war, especially between American and British officials and bankers, strengthened this bond, which became even more pronounced in the 1920s, 1930s and, of course, during the experience of the Second World War.[301]

This community of interests served as the basis for the famed "special relationship," the belief that shared language, basic political principles and common international objectives bind the United States and Britain together. The belief, born during the First World War, emerged in full form during its aftermath and, while promoted in the United States by such figures as Harry Davison, seemed most attractive to British business and political leaders. Indeed, the latter were motivated by the sense that Britain was in relative decline in comparison with the burgeoning economic and potential military clout of the United States.

But there were deeper currents at work as well. The most significant of these was an instinctive sense of class and ethnic solidarity—both inbred and learned—which affected virtually all the major players in the New York financial and business world and underlay the calculations in most governmental decisions.

The prep school–Ivy League path, the "cursus honorum" for the American elite at the time, could legitimately boast many genuine attributes as well as advantages for its members. The curriculum emphasizing classics, literature, languages and philosophy fostered mental discipline and disseminated the richness of western knowledge (despised and condemned in some quarters today). As taught, understood and accepted (despite the more critical work of progressive historians such as Charles Beard), history was highly patriotic, Eurocentric and assumed imperialism by the white western powers, domestically and internationally, as both normal and positive. Those who enjoyed travel opportunities or exposure to other cultures through business and/or governmental contacts might develop a more nuanced appreciation of such things. Or not.

Additionally, by the late nineteenth century, earlier wariness and dislike of Britain and its global reach was fading in the intellectual and financial bastions of the United States as the establishment of an overseas American empire, regardless of how limited, engendered a more sympathetic, if not idealized, view of British global conquest and colonization.

Indeed, Geoffrey Hodgson's description of Henry Stimson is applicable to any number of up-and-coming elite power players who would influence, and often direct, events during and after World War I. Stimson was, Hodgson writes, always in touch with "men who believed like him, that the time had come when America's role in the world should match her strength and her convictions. Stimson was a disciple of those men, Elihu Root, Leonard Wood, and above all Theodore Roosevelt," who envisioned America as the new global power—playing Rome to Britain's Greece.[302]

But there was more. The young men of Long Island's—and the nation's—wealthiest communities were themselves almost all of British stock and saw in themselves, a reflection, possibly even more advanced, of their British counterparts. This attitude was driven home, at least in an implied fashion, through their educational experiences. Nor were they likely to run across many not of their background and who shared their assumptions in the prep schools and colleges of their time. Catholics would have been few and far between, partly because they were discouraged by their own churchmen from attending secular schools, which still maintained a Protestant ethos, and partly because they were discriminated against through admission policies. Jews were similarly a rare sight in such settings.[303] Consequently, the entire educational process from prep school through college, and often beyond, inculcated a sense of Anglo-Saxon solidarity and supremacy and an unchallenged assumption that the mores, standards and political objectives of their class were the desirable—indeed national—norm.[304]

Experiences after college did little to alter such convictions. If the prep schools were feeders for the Ivies, they, in turn, supplied the abundance of young talent for the leading law firms in New York and Boston, and these dominated the pool of upper-echelon officials in the federal government.

The assumptions, biases and standards that were absorbed through such experiences—the patrician WASP world view—was reinforced by the social milieu the leading financial/business and legal families created. Clustered in estate communities among those of their background, a human predilection, they founded or joined the same clubs, both in the city and on Long Island. The clubs—whose membership was controlled by member approval as well as steep fees—also promoted a similarity of outlook, confidence in their status and security in their belief that their prescriptions for the nation and world were correct.

From these habits of mind, fostered through educational background, wealth and social and political homogeneity, emerged the agenda that drove policy and action regarding the world war and the American role in the conflict. These assumptions and interests, when activated, helped prepare the nation for war once it came. But they also undercut the pursuit—or even genuine consideration—of any alternative policy and inexorably set the United States on a course that made war with Germany inevitable.

# RICH LEGACY

*T*he Gold Coast today, the North Shore between Kings Point and (depending on one's criteria) Setauket or Port Jefferson, is significantly reduced in both overall area and number of estates. Continuing the pre-1914 trend, high-end country houses continued to be built at a healthy rate during the 1920s, with wealthy newcomers such as Marshall Field and Vincent Astor (both First World War veterans) adding their residences to the area's treasury of distinguished houses and grounds. Not surprisingly, construction declined precipitously during the Great Depression, and estate construction came to a virtual end with World War II.

Even with the resumption of more prosperous times, steep property taxes, income taxes, rising construction costs and changing tastes in architecture and lifestyle put an end to the large country house era on Long Island and elsewhere. Financial pressures and changing fashions led newer owners, who often inherited the properties from parents and grandparents, to sell off portions or even all of their holdings. Some estates fell into severe neglect and disrepair as owners died without heirs or moved away without providing funds for upkeep. Consequently, large swaths of land formerly dominated by great country houses and gardens were turned into suburban housing. Others fell victim to fire, vandalism and default.

But not all was lost. Of the over 1,000 country house estates estimated standing in the 1910–30 period, 574 were extant by the 1980s; 424 were still residences, with the remainder repurposed in a variety of roles.[305] Some were acquired by the counties or state with uneven results in terms of upkeep and use. Others became arboretums, colleges or religious houses.

Despite considerable losses, much of the Gold Coast survives, at least in its physical aspects. The area's creators, the wealthy owners, not to mention their architects, landscape designers and armies of workers and servants, left a rich legacy to Long Island, its people and the region. With some knowledge of the area and careful selection of roadways, it is possible to design a driving or biking tour from the estate areas of Kings Point, detour quickly via 25a to Port Washington Boulevard and drive north to the low-density, high-income sections of Sands Point, the peninsula where Fitzgerald's Daisy Buchanan lured the doomed Jay Gatsby. It is another quick dip to 25a and then another drive north to Glen Cove, Lattingtown, Center Island and Mill Neck, areas retaining a rich collection of vintage and more recent estates and country houses. If the explorer is not yet sated, he or she might take a short jaunt through the village of Oyster Bay and into Oyster Bay Cove, where Sagamore Hill still commands views of the bay and Sound, looking much as it did when Theodore Roosevelt lived there.

There's more. From Oyster Bay, proceed east again on 25a toward Huntington before turning north into Lloyd Harbor. This process can be repeated eastward into Nisseqougue, Head of the Harbor and Old Field until the driver has neared Port Jefferson.

Nor is all the Gold Coast confined to the necks of land protruding into Long Island Sound. Planning a more southerly route south of Glen Cove, an estate tourist can enjoy the landscapes and architecture of the Brookvilles and ultimately Old Westbury. For maximum enjoyment and considerations of time, such excursions are best handled in sections, as each component of the Gold Coast deserves adequate time. Some places offer attractions enough to require a day to themselves.

What the driver, bicyclist or even hiker will experience is much of the most distinguished architecture and grounds remaining on Long Island. That it survives for the enjoyment of all, at least visually, is the legacy, intended or not, of the 1880–1930 generations and the measures they and their descendants took to ensure the survival of their handiwork. Additionally, preservation groups and historical societies have taken an active role in calling attention to the beauty and significance of many endangered estates, thus preventing many losses of important buildings and landscapes. As a result, significant sections of the Gold Coast retain sizable remnants of the natural flora and fauna, woods, wetlands, creeks and shoreline.

Westbury House, former home of Jay Phipps and now the centerpiece of Old Westbury Gardens. Constructed in 1905–7, it is open to the public. *Courtesy of the Collections of Old Westbury Gardens.*

While the prices of the remaining houses and estates are beyond the reach of most, anyone can enjoy the sight of landscaped gardens, specimen trees and some of the most impressive architecture existing in the United States. While most sites can be seen only from roadways, a number of Gold Coast estates, houses and grounds are open to the public and can be experienced more fully and leisurely. Old Westbury Gardens, Coe Hall/Planting Felds Arboretum, Welwyn, Caumsett State Park (the Marshall Field estate) and W.K. Vanderbilt's Eagles' Nest are among the major estates open to the public.

The extant Gold Coast constitutes a cultural and environmental legacy to Long Island, the region and the nation. It is a rich one in all senses of the word.

# NOTES

## *Chapter 1*

1. Robert B. MacKay traces the Gold Coast era further back to the end of the Civil War, though the Gold Coast distinctiveness visibly began to assume its familiar character in the 1880s. MacKay, Baker and Traynor, *Long Island Country Houses*, 19.
2. Roberts, "First World War as Catalyst and Epiphany," 321.
3. MacKay, Baker and Traynor, *Long Island Country Houses*, 19.
4. Ibid.
5. Ibid.
6. "Country Life in America" (February 1920), 30, in MacKay, Baker and Traynor, *Long Island Country Houses*, 17.
7. Lamont, *Henry P. Davison*, 241.
8. Ibid.
9. Ibid., 240. The estate was left to his eldest son, Trubee, at his death in 1922, with the idea that it would remain as a gathering place for the family. Indeed, Davison built homes for Trubee and his daughter Alice and their families on the grounds. Peacock Point remains with the Davison family to this day.
10. MacKay, Baker and Traynor, *Long Island Country Houses*, 32.

## *Chapter 2*

11. Cited in Chernow, *House of Morgan*, 186.

12. Pietrusza, *TR's Last War*, 201.

13. Chernow, *House of Morgan*, 130.

14. Lamont, *Henry P. Davison*, 323.

15. Ibid., 173.

16. Ibid., 329. This, of course, overlooked or ignored the non-Anglo-Saxon segment of the American population, which contained large blocs of noninterventionists as well as many groups, German and Irish Americans who were cynical if not hostile to the Allies. Davison stuck by his Anglo-Saxon supremacy convictions until the end. His friend and colleague Lamont remembered he believed a "stable peace could be attained only through the efforts of these two [U.S. and UK] Anglo-Saxon peoples working shoulder to shoulder."

17. Ibid., 7.

18. Koistinen, *Mobilizing for Modern War*, 118.

19. Some researchers contend that the "partners at JP Morgan conceived of the Allied cause as the British cause, a perspective that led them to rebuff calls for greater Franco-American co-operation." Martin Horn, "A Private Bank at War: JP Morgan & Co. and France, 1914–1918," *Business History Review* 74 (Spring 2000): 85.

20. Koistinen, *Mobilizing for Modern War*, 119.

21. Roberts, "First World War as Catalyst and Epiphany," 321.

22. Koistinen, *Mobilizing for Modern War*, 129.

23. Ibid., 128–29.

24. Roberts, "First World War as Catalyst and Epiphany," 321.

25. An associate who had accompanied Davison on one of his overseas trips described him as "a little too inclined to think he's in a story book and to be a little too conscious that he is on very intimate terms with chancellors and P.M.s and things." He himself wrote of "Never hav[ing] such an interesting experience" and implying he was the right man to represent the Morgan Bank in London "during this period of stress and abnormal conditions." Ibid., 323.

26. Ibid., 325.

27. Ibid.

28. Ibid., 326.

29. Ibid.

30. Koistinen, *Mobilizing for Modern War*, 132.

31. British financial secretary Sir Harman Lever thought that much of the problem with the Federal Reserve Board "stemmed from Henry P. Davison's handling of its members." Dayer, "Strange Bedfellows," 133.

32. Dayer, "Strange Bedfellows," 132. See also Roberts, "First World War as Catalyst and Epiphany," 328.

33. Roberts, "First World War as Catalyst and Epiphany," 326.

34. Ibid.

35. Ibid.

36. Morgan reluctantly financed British purchases by extending Britain a demand loan, similar to running a bar tab. The most thorough examination of Morgan Bank machinations during the Great War can be found in Koistinen's *Mobilizing for Modern War*, and I have relied heavily on it in this section. For British dependence on American supplies, see Wagner, *America and the Great War*, 142–43. In autumn 1917, the British Board of Trade reported to the government that "for numerous articles, America is an absolutely irreplaceable source of supply."

37. Koistinen, *Mobilizing for Modern War*, 135. The discharge of Allied debt to the United States was a matter of some complexity, especially as measures were taken to conceal it from the public and even Congress. The federal government, often through Liberty Loan funds, paid off the $400 million British Demand loan, mostly held by Morgan, and American dollars satisfied British international debt. Again, the most complete, detailed and exhaustively researched account is found in Koistinen.

38. Dayer, "Strange Bedfellows," 150. After Davison accepted the role of national Red Cross coordinator, Lamont became the key player at Morgan. It was he who acted as financial advisor to the American delegation at the Paris Peace Conference.

39. Lamont deemed Davison's concentrating of Allied purchases of war materials with the Morgan Bank the greatest of his accomplishments. Lamont, *Henry P. Davison*, 217.

40. Forbes, *Stettinius, Sr.*, 31.

41. Ibid., 48.

42. Ibid., 57.

43. Ibid., 100.

44. Chernow, *House of Morgan*, 189.

45. Forbes, *Stettinius, Sr.*, 52.

46. Ibid., 50–51.

47. Koistinen, *Mobilizing for Modern War*, 121.

48. Chernow, *House of Morgan*, 189. For the full mechanics of this loan, which was actually made in cloaked British money, see Koistinen, *Mobilizing for Modern War*, 136–37.

49. Ibid., 123.

50. The boom had its negative effects, creating distortions in the American economy. Chief among these was inflation caused by the massive shipping of goods to Europe, decreasing domestic supply and causing coal, meat and sugar shortages in the United States. Some have argued that this economic situation could not be sustained and that intervention in one form or another was becoming necessary to stabilize the domestic situation. See Wawro, *Sons of Freedom*, 43–46.

51. Ibid., 124.

52. Chernow, *House of Morgan*, 188.

53. Stettinius complained at the time that the public "will never know and, if it did know probably would never believe what sacrifices of profit JP Morgan and Company and the members of that firm have made in acting for the Governments....It is a damnable outrage that men whose standards are as high as the members of that firm are so calumated and abused by some of the papers in the country." Cited in Forbes, *Stettinius, Sr.*, 61.

54. *Brooklyn Eagle*, July 4, 1915, 4.

55. Daniel E. Russell, "The Day Morgan Was Shot," Glen Cove Public Library, unpaginated. Russell was city historian of Glen Cove and curator of Glen Cove's Local History Room in the 1970s and 1980s. His is the most detailed account of the assault on Morgan and his household. Unfortunately, Russell did not cite his sources, though it is clear that he drew most of his information from newspaper accounts both regional and local.

56. *Brooklyn Eagle*, July 4, 1915, 4.

57. Ibid.

58. Russell, "The Day Morgan Was Shot."

59. *Brooklyn Eagle*, July 4, 1915, 4.

60. *New York Times*, July 7, 1915, 1.

61. Ibid., 2.

62. Russell, "The Day Morgan Was Shot."

63. Ibid.

64. *New York Times*, July 7, 1915, 2.

65. Ibid.

66. Ibid., 3.

67. *Brooklyn Eagle*, July 4, 1915, 4.
68. Russell, "The Day Morgan Was Shot."
69. *New York Times*, July 7, 1915, 1; July 9, 1915.
70. Ibid., July 8, 1915, 1; April 13, 1916, 4.
71. Russell, "The Day Morgan Was Shot."
72. *New York Times*, July 10, 1915, 1.
73. Ibid.
74. Russell, "The Day Morgan Was Shot."
75. Ibid.
76. Blum, *Dark Invasion*, 101.
77. Ibid., 412.
78. Ibid., 101.
79. Ibid., 275.
80. Ibid.
81. Russell, "The Day Morgan Was Shot."
82. *New York Times*, July 10, 1915, 2.

## Chapter 3

83. Renehan, *Lion's Pride*, 82–83.
84. Ibid.
85. *Brooklyn Eagle*, June 6, 1917, 7.
86. Wortman, *Millionaire's Unit*, 6.
87. Renehan, *Lion's Pride*, 81; *Brooklyn Eagle*, September 26, 1914, 6.
88. *Brooklyn Eagle*, April 14, 1915, 22.
89. Doenecke, *Nothing Less Than Victory*, 187.
90. Ibid.
91. Wagner, *America and the Great War*, 88.
92. *New York Times*, October 3, 1916, 24. He added that "many manufacturers had not made much," and "I could name some who have actually lost by [munitions contracts]." Such firms were likely not on Stettinius's list of preferred manufacturers. Morgan and its allies were profiting immensely.
93. Andrew Bacevich, "The Odds Against Antiwar Warriors," *American Conservative*, March 30, 2017, theamericanconservative.co/articles/the-odds-against-antiwar-warriors.
94. Morris, *Colonel Roosevelt*, 421.
95. Ibid., 429.

96. In a recent study, Philip Zelikow argues that the major belligerents on the Western Front, Germany, France and Britain, sought Wilson's mediation to bring the war to an end in autumn 1916. Britain's interest was especially driven by the specter of immediate bankruptcy. Zelikow, *Road Less Traveled.*

97. Wood had initiated summer training camps before the war in 1913. It was not, however, until 1915 that the movement gathered steam under the impetus of pro-Allied college students. See Schaffer, *America in the Great War*, 186.

98. Some older Preparedness activists attended as well, including Robert Bacon; Henry Stimson, Taft's secretary of war and a resident of Huntington; and John Purroy Mitchell, mayor of New York. But it was the young men and students who dominated.

99. Pietrusza, *TR's Last War*, 62.

100. *Brooklyn Eagle*, August 25, 1915, 1.

101. The distinctly eastern, affluent character of the Preparedness-interventionist movement was noted by former secretary of state William Jennings Bryan, who toured the country denouncing "Eastern aristocrats with fomenting a war in which Midwestern farmers and machinists would do most of the dying." Renehan, *Lion's Pride*, 105.

102. *Quarterly Journal of the Great War Society* 6, no. 4 (Autumn 1997).

103. Clifford, *Citizen Soldiers*, 189.

104. Ibid.

105. Pietrusza, *TR's Last War*, 196.

106. Ibid.

107. Ibid. 198.

108. Doenecke, *Nothing Less Than Victory*, 113.

109. Ibid.

110. Cited in Morris, *Colonel Roosevelt*, 433.

111. *Brooklyn Eagle*, March 31, 1916, 4.

112. Ibid.

113. Robert Bacon was president of the National Security League.

114. Pietruzsa, *TR's Last War*, 92.

115. *Brooklyn Eagle*, May 7, 1916, 6.

116. Ibid., April 30, 1916, 24.

117. Ibid.

118. Pietruzsa, *TR's Last War*, 76–77.

119. Ibid.

120. Hodgson, *The Colonel*, 171.

121. Ibid.
122. *New York Times*, December 16, 1914, 5.
123. Hodgson, *The Colonel*, 83.
124. *Brooklyn Eagle*, December 9, 1915, 1.
125. Ibid.
126. Ibid.
127. *New York Times*, January 31, 1916, 4.
128. Ibid., February 8, 1916, 10.
129. *Brooklyn Eagle*, December 5, 1916, 4.
130. Ibid., February 2, 28; 1917, 8.
131. Back in New York ten days after the declaration of war, Stimson told reporters that "enthusiasm for France was the most marked feature of the trip." Even more reassuring was his statement that "we have conferred with many prominent German-Americans in communities where they formed a large percentage of the population. In many cases they are men who prior to America's declaration of war were strongly against the Allies. We found them unreservedly loyal to the United States." *New York Times*, April 16, 1917, 5.
132. Wortman, *Millionaire's Unit*, 44.
133. *Brooklyn Eagle*, November 14, 1916, 8.
134. Ibid.
135. *New York Times*, June 9, 1916, 13.
136. Ibid., November 29, 1916, 5.
137. Ibid.
138. Ibid.
139. Wagner, *Millionaire's Unit*, 106.

## *Chapter 4*

140. *New York Times*, March 22, 1917, 7.
141. Ibid.
142. See Hodgson, *The Colonel*, 43.
143. *New York Times*, March 22, 1917, 17.
144. Ibid., May 5, 1917, 13.
145. Ibid.
146. Ibid.
147. Ibid.
148. Hodgson, *The Colonel*, 84.

149. Ibid.

150. *New York Times*, May 27, 1917, 2.

151. Ibid.

152. Wortman, *Millionaire's Unit*, 115–16. Wortman argues that Trubee had experienced some sort of panic attack, which led to his accident.

153. *New York Times*, August 9, 1921, 7.

154. Pietrusza, *TR's Last War*, 165.

155. Collier with Horowitz, *Roosevelts*, 195.

156. Renehan, *Lion's Pride*, 132.

157. Ibid.

158. Ibid., 154.

159. *New York Times*, August 4, 1917, 6.

160. Ibid.

161. Ibid.

162. Renehan, *Lion's Pride*, 165.

163. *Brooklyn Eagle*, October 5, 1917, 4.

164. Davison, "First Yale Naval Aero Unit," in Nettleson, *Yale in the World War*, 443.

165. Boegner and Gachot, *Halcyon Days*, 107.

166. Ibid., December 15, 1918, 4.

167. Ibid.

168. Ibid.

169. Homberger, *Mrs. Astor's New York*, 207.

170. Letter, Helen Phipps Martin, August 10, 1917, collections of Old Westbury Gardens.

171. *New York Tribune*, June 17, 1918, 9.

172. *New York Times*, April 15, 1917, xi.

173. Ibid., August 8, 1916, 7.

174. *Brooklyn Eagle*, September 15, 1917, 16.

## *Chapter 5*

175. *New York Times*, May 30, 1917, 11.

176. Ibid., May 4, 1917, 10.

177. Ibid., May 30, 1917, 11.

178. Ibid., June 17, 1917, 19.

179. Ibid.

180. Publicity release, Rosemary Farm Red Cross Festival, September 1917, Huntington Historical Society.
181. Ibid.
182. *Long Islander*, October 12, 1917, 1.
183. *Vogue*, November 15, 1917, oldlongisland.com/2009/05/rosemary-farm-national-red-cross-html.
184. Ibid. The pageant, minus the outdoor ambiance, was repeated at the Metropolitan Opera in November.
185. *New York Times*, June 16, 1918, 28.
186. Ibid., June 30, 1918, 17.
187. Ibid.
188. *New York Tribune*, June 29, 1918, 11.
189. Wooley, "Davison Estate in War Time," 42.
190. Ibid., 39–41.
191. *Brooklyn Eagle*, October 13, 1917, 3.
192. Ibid.
193. *New York Times*, March 31, 1917, 16.
194. Ibid., September 30, 1918, B7.
195. Ibid., August 5, 1917, B7.
196. Lamont, *Henry P. Davison*, 267.
197. Roberts, "First World War as Catalyst and Epiphany,"328.
198. Ibid., 331.
199. Ibid.
200. Lamont, *Henry P. Davison*, 269.
201. Ibid.
202. Ibid., 11.
203. Ibid., 294.

## Chapter 6

204. *New York Times*, August 18, 1918, 14.
205. Renehan, *Lion's Pride*, 185.
206. Ibid.
207. Ibid., 149.
208. Dick Derby, *New York Times*, April 1, 1918, 20.
209. Pietrusza, *TR's Last War*, 234.
210. Ibid., 244.

211. Renehan, *Lion's Pride*, 206.

212. Morris, *Colonel Roosevelt*, 528.

213. Ibid., 529.

214. Ibid., 532.

215. Collier with Horowitz, *Roosevelts*, 242.

216. Hodgson, *The Colonel*, 84.

217. Ibid., 85.

218. Bruce Huffman, "Long Due Tribute Rendered," *Daedalus Flyer*, Fall 2017, 6.

219. Ibid.

220. Ibid.

221. Ibid.

222. Ibid., 7.

223. *Brooklyn Eagle*, February 14, 1918, 18.

224. Ibid.

225. Washington *Evening Star*, February 19, 1918, 10.

226. Ibid.

227. *New York Times*, February 14, 1918, 3.

228. *Brooklyn Eagle*, March 16, 1918, 3.

229. *New York Herald*, April 28, 1918, 2.

230. *Brooklyn Eagle*, November 18, 1918, 8.

231. *New York Times*, September 9, 1918.

232. *Brooklyn Eagle*, September 30, 1918, 4; November 15, 1918, 18.

233. Ibid., December 8, 1918, 55. Hitchcock's comments on the meager monotony of German prisoner food were echoed by American prisoners of war in World War II. The Germans provided potato bread, *blutwurst* (blood pudding) and soup, which was generally all they had available. The diet might have been adequate for survival, but not much else. Food packages from International Red Cross contained greater variety, more calories and small treats such as chocolate and cigarettes. Consequently, the arrival of such packages was highly anticipated and greatly appreciated by the temporary residents of the *Stalags*.

234. *New York Times*, May 1, 1918, 3.

235. *Brooklyn Eagle*, July 16, 1918, 12.

236. *New York Times*, October 5, 1918, 1.

237. Forbes, *Stettinius, Sr.*, 101.

238. Geoffrey Wawro, *Sons of Freedom*, 429.

239. Ibid., 508.

240. Ibid., 411.

241. Ibid., 394.
242. Ibid.
243. Letter, J.S. Morgan to Admiral Sir Lewis Bayly RN, February 10, 1934, Old Westbury Gardens Collections.
244. Classes of 1888 and 1889, Princeton University, 19.
245. OWG material, source unknown.
246. Classes of 1888 and 1889, 19.
247. Ibid. The United States had fewer military decorations in the Great War period than it currently confers, and regulations for award were different than today. Since World War II, the Navy Cross has been awarded only for gallantry in combat against an enemy. It is the navy and marine corps equivalent of the army/air force Distinguished Service Cross. The Distinguished Service Cross (awarded in World War I) and the Navy Cross are second to the Medal of Honor in decorations of bravery.

## Chapter 7

248. Roberts, "First World War as Catalyst and Epiphany," 318.
249. Ibid., 331.
250. Ibid.
251. Ibid.
252. Ibid., 335.
253. Ibid., 337.
254. Forbes, *Stettinius, Sr.*, 110.
255. Ibid., 111.
256. *New York Times*, February 14, 1919, 12.
257. Ibid., October 20, 1960, 1.
258. Forbes, *Stettinius, Sr.*, 90. In the same year, Stettinius donated $50,000 to various charities (all numbers in 1920 dollars).
259. Ibid., 199. The project cost Stettinius $109,779.87, which was to be repaid over time by the Locust Valley Cemetery Association.
260. *New York Times*, May 5, 1922, 1.
261. *New York Times*, March 12, 1925, 4.
262. Ibid.
263. Ibid., May 10, 1922, 12.
264. Ibid.
265. Lamont, *Henry P. Davison*, 329.
266. *New York Times*, April 25, 1925, 1.

267. Ibid.

268. Ibid.

269. Trubee tore down the house his father had built before the war and built a new one for himself and his wife, the former Dorothy Peabody (1899–1992). His two sisters and their families also lived in separate houses on the estate, which became a Davison family compound. Spinzia and Spinzia, *Long Island's Prominent North Shore Families*, 190.

270. *New York Times*, November 14, 1974, 34.

271. Harry Jr. built his own home in Upper Brookville, a short drive south from Lattingtown. Called Appledore, it is now the Mill River Club.

272. *New York Times*, July 3, 1961, 15.

273. Forbes, *Stettinius, Sr.*, 205.

274. Ibid., 230.

275. He was not buried there immediately. Following the funeral service, his body was taken to a holding vault at the Memorial Cemetery at Cold Spring Harbor while a mausoleum was planned for his grave at Locust Valley. Such a memorial was never built, and both Stettinius and his wife rest under large grave slabs.

276. *New York Times*, September 4, 1925, 21.

277. Lamont, *Henry P. Davison*, 230.

278. *New York Times*, March 13, 1943, 1.

279. Ibid., October 20, 1960, 1.

280. Ibid., August 11, 1980.

281. *New York Times*, October 20, 1960, 1.

282. Ibid., November 10, 1944, 2.

283. Collier with Horowitz, *Roosevelts*, 290–91.

284. Ibid., 337.

285. Ibid., 410.

286. *New York Times*, June 4, 1963, 39.

287. Ibid., April 20, 1944, 4. See also www.brittanica.com/Thomas Hitchcock-Jr.

288. Ibid.

289. Aldrich, *American Hero*, 266.

290. *Newsday*, July 11, 1945, 23.

291. Ibid.

292. Forbes, *Stettinius, Sr.*, x.

293. *New York Times*, December 19, 1918, 5.

294. Stimson did similar duty at a ceremony honoring returning veterans at Huntington's Presbyterian Church. *Brooklyn Eagle*, December 1, 1919, 4.

295. Ibid., November 30, 1919, 6.

296. Though he did push up the date of the games from Thanksgiving to Columbus Day. Hodgson, *The Colonel*, 175.

297. Citation of Presentation Read by President Truman at the Presentation of the Distinguished Service Medal to Henry L. Stimson, September 21, 1945, Huntington Historical Society.

298. Hodgson, *The Colonel*, 170.

299. *Long Islander*, September 25, 1947, 1.

300. Following his death, Highhold was given to the Boy Scouts as an activity center. The main house was torn down, though the original farmhouse that was on the site when Stimson first bought the land remains. The grounds are now a Suffolk County park. St. John's Memorial Cemetery is actually in Laurel Hollow, though the church that owns it is in Cold Spring Harbor.

## Chapter 8

301. Hodgson, *The Colonel*, 173. Hodgson writes, "The First World War… not only imbued the political and business elites in London and New York with a new comradeship, forged on the battlefield, or at least wartime committee rooms, but it had made the British highly conscious of their relative economic and military power." True, but the shared sense of Anglo-Saxon identity and natural right to leadership preceded 1914 among the eastern financial and business elites, though the dominant role in the partnership was altered by the American role in the war.

302. Ibid., 203. Renehan reached a similar conclusion. Writing of TR and Lodge, his words are applicable to the politically activated Long Island elite. They were "the first generation of an eastern upper-class network of individuals educated at the Big Three Colleges [Harvard Yale and Princeton] and law schools and entrenched in the Wall Street law firms and major banks. Strategically located at the heart of the economy and endowed with the advantages of genteel birth, this elite constated…the most highly developed and powerful sector of the American public."

303. Stimson harbored a bias against Columbia University due to its "tremendous Jewish influence." Hodgson, *The Colonel*, 373.

304. Roberts applies the term "Atlanticist" to the agenda of WASP power players to secure Anglo-American dominance in Europe and elsewhere. Its origins were rooted in the fact that "most Americans who belonged

to the Northeastern patrician elite subscribed almost unthinkingly to beliefs in Anglo-Saxon racial superiority and the strategic desirability of Anglo-American cooperation." Roberts, "First World War as Catalyst and Epiphany," 317.

## Appendix

305. MacKay, Baker and Traynor, *Long Island Country Houses*, 33.

# BIBLIOGRAPHY

*Brooklyn Eagle*
*New York Times*
*Old Westbury Gardens*. Miscellaneous Papers.


Aldrich, Nelson, Jr. *American Hero: The True Story of Tommy Hitchcock*. Guilford, CT: Lyons Press, 2016.

Blum, Howard. *Dark Invasion: 1915 Germany's Secret War and the Hunt for the First Terrorist Cell in America*. New York: HarperCollins, 2014

Boegner, Peggy Phipps, and Richard Gachot. *Halcyon Days: An American Family through Three Generations*. New York: Old Westbury Gardens and Abrams, 2007.

Chernow, Ron. *The House of Morgan: An American Banking Dynasty and the Rise of Modern Finance*. New York: Touchstone Books, 1990.

Clifford, John Garry. *The Citizen Soldiers: The Plattsburg Training Camp Movement, 1913–1920*. Lexington: University of Kentucky Press, 1972.

Collier, Peter, with David Horwitz. *The Roosevelts: An American Saga*. New York: Simon and Schuster, 1994.

Davison, Trubee F. "The First Yale Naval Aviation Unit." In *Yale in the World War*, edited by George Henry Nettleson. 2 vols. New Haven, CT: Yale University Press, 1925. Vol. 1, 443–48.

Dayer, Roberta A. "Strange Bedfellows: J.P. Morgan & Co., Whitehall and the Wilson Administration During World War I." *Business History* 18, no. 2 (1976): 127–51.

Doenecke, Justus B. *Nothing Less Than Victory*. Lexington: University of Kentucky Press, 2011.

Forbes, John Douglas. *Stettinius, Sr.: Portrait of a Morgan Partner*. Charlottesville: University of Virginia Press, 1974.

Hodgson, Godfrey. *The Colonel: The Life and Wars of Henry Stimson, 1867–1950*. New York: Alfred A. Knopf, 1990.

Homberger, Eric. *Mrs. Astor's New York: Money and Social Power in a Gilded Age*. New Haven, CT: Yale University Press, 2002.

Koistinen, Paul A. *Mobilizing for Modern War: The Political Economy of American Warfare, 1865–1919*. Lawrence: University of Kansas Press, 1997.

Lamont, Edward M. *The Ambassador from Wall Street: The Story of Thomas W. Lamont*. Lantham, MD: Madison Books, 1994.

Lamont, Thomas W. *Henry P. Davison: The Record of a Useful Life*. New York: Harper and Brothers, 1933.

MacKay, Robert B., Anthony Baker and Carol Traynor, eds. *Long Island Country Houses and Their Architects, 1860–1940*. New York: Society for the Preservation of Long Island Antiquities in Association with W.W. Norton, 1997.

Morris, Edmund. *Colonel Roosevelt*. New York: Random House, 2010.

Pietrusza, David. *TR's Last War: Theodore Roosevelt, the Great War, and a Journey of Triumph and Tragedy*. Guilford, CT: Lyons Press, 2018.

Renehan, Edward J. *The Lion's Pride: Theodore Roosevelt and His Family in War and Peace*. New York: Oxford University Press, 1998.

Roberts, Priscilla. "The First World War as Catalyst and Epiphany: The Case of Henry P. Davison." *Diplomacy and Statecraft* 20 (June 2007): 315–50.

Schaffer, Ronald. *America in the Great War: The Rise of the Welfare State*. New York: Oxford University Press, 1991.

Spinzia, Raymond E., and Judith A. Spinzia. *Long Island's Prominent North Shore Families: Their Estates and Their Country Homes*. Vol. 1. College Station, TX: Virtual Bookworm, 2006.

Wagner, Margaret E. *America and the Great War*. New York: Bloomsbury USA, 2017.

Wawro, Geoffrey. *Sons of Freedom: The Forgotten American Soldiers Who Defeated Germany in World War I*. New York: Basic Books, 2018.

Welch, Richard F. *Long Island and World War I*. Charleston, SC: The History Press, 2018.

Wooley, Edward Mott. "The Davison Estate in War Time." *The New Country Life*, August 1918, 39–42.

Wortman, Marc. *The Millionaire's Unit: The Aristocratic Flyboys Who Fought the Great War and Invented American Air Power*. New York: Public Affairs, 2006.

Zelikow, Philip. *The Road Less Traveled: The Secret Battle to End the Great War, 1916–1917*. New York: Public Affairs, 2021.

# INDEX

# About the Author

A Long Island native, Richard F. Welch received his doctorate in American history from Stony Brook University. He taught United States history, western civilization, Irish history and American military history at Long Island University and Farmingdale State College. Dr. Welch's work has appeared in the *Long Island Historical Journal*, *Journal of the American Revolution*, *America's Civil War*, *Civil War Times*, *Military History*, *American History* and the *New York Times*. He is also the author of six books, including *The Boy General: The Life and Careers of Francis Channing Barlow*, *General Washington's Commando: Benjamin Tallmadge in the American Revolution* and *Long Island and World War I*. He also serves on the board of directors of the Suffolk County Historical Society. He resides in Northport, Long Island, New York.

*Visit us at*
www.historypress.com